Kids' London

Kids' London

by

Elizabeth Holt & Molly Perham

Illustrated by David McKee

Abelard-Schuman

London

Printed in Great Britain

ISBN 0 200 71916 5 (paperback)
ISBN 0 200 71924 6 (hardback)

Abelard-Schuman Limited
158 Buckingham Palace Road
London SW1

24 Market Square
Aylesbury Bucks

Contents

How To Use This Book

This book was written for two very different groups of people, Londoners, and London visitors.

Londoners are, on the whole, blind. Perhaps because there is so much on their doorstep, they tend to take everything for granted. Once they've seen the traditional sights they forget how much more is available for them. So, for Londoners, we have tried to suggest things they might otherwise overlook and to show how many exciting and interesting things there are for them to do.

Although visitors might feel envious because this guide mentions places like canoeing centres and multimedia projects, we have tried to make it possible for them to look at London in a different way.

Everyone knows how good the museums are, but it soon becomes exhausting plodding round one after the other, so we have taken topics like clocks, costumes and armour and suggested some of the best places to see them. With the help of a Red Rover the opportunities are limitless.

To make the guide easier to use, museums, centres and organisations are in the index in the back together with their opening and closing times and bus and tube directions. These might vary and you would be wise to check them so that you don't have a wasted journey.

Of course, London has so much to offer that it is quite impossible to include everything in one book. If we have left out things that you yourself particularly enjoy, why not let us know about it so that we can bear it in mind for future books?

Daily Ceremonies

Ceremony of the Keys
This takes place every evening at 21.40 when the Chief Warder of the Tower of London, escorted by the Brigade of Guards, locks the Middle, West and Byward Tower Gates. You can only see this if you have the written permission of the Governor.

Changing of the Guard (Buckingham Palace)
The new guard, accompanied by a band, marches from either Chelsea or Wellington barracks to change the guard in a traditional ceremony that takes about half an hour. It is held at 11.30.

Changing of the Guard (St James's Palace)
The old guard leaves St James's Palace for Buckingham Palace at 11.15 daily. This is a ceremony which takes a very short time to perform.

Changing of the Life Guards (Horse Guards)
This ceremony which lasts about 20 minutes takes place from Monday-Saturday at 11.00. On Sunday it occurs at 10.00. There is a daily inspection of the guard at 16.00 every day.

Recognising Uniforms

Bank of England

Gate-keepers	Scarlet and gold gowns
Messengers	Pink coats, scarlet waistcoats

Chelsea Pensioners

Summer	Scarlet frock-coats
Winter	Dark blue tunics

Guards

Coldstream	Bearskin with scarlet plume on right
Grenadier	Bearskin with white goat-hair plume on left
Irish	Bearskin with pale blue feather on right
Scots	Bearskin with no decoration
Welsh	Bearskin with white and green feather plume on left

Household Cavalry

Blues and Royals	Blue tunics, red plumed helmets
Life Guards	Scarlet tunics, white plumed helmets

King's Troop, Royal Horse

Artillery	Blue hussar-type jacket with piped gold braid, red striped breeches

Royal Bodyguard

Gentlemen-at-Arms	Scarlet tail-coats, gold epaulettes, white gauntlets, gold-striped trousers, Wellington boots, gilt helmets with long swans' feathers. Swords and sticks for officers; swords and pole-axes for gentlemen
Yeomen of the Guard	Tudor costume of scarlet, trimmed with black and gold, white ruffs, red stockings, red and white rosettes on shoes, garlanded flat hat. Waist and crossbelt
Yeomen Warders	Identical to Yeomen of the Guard but without the crossbelt

Calendar

January

Racing and Sporting Motor-Cycle Show	Horticultural Hall
Boat Show	Earl's Court
Presentation of a boar's head on a silver platter to the Lord Mayor by the Butchers' Company and a lamb by the Tenants' Association. This is a ceremony which dates from the 12th Century	Smithfield
Model Engineer Exhibition	Seymour Hall
Royal Academy Winter Exhibition	Burlington House
City of London Art Exhibition	Guildhall
Cutting of the Baddeley Cake. Robert Baddeley left money to an actors' fund as well as £100 to spend on a cake and punch for twelfth night. This is meant for actors and their friends but if you are really interested in the theatre try writing to the Trustees of the Baddeley Fund, 6 Adam Street, WC2 for admission	Drury Lane Theatre
Royal Epiphany Gifts of gold, frankincense and myrrh offered by gentlemen-ushers on behalf of the Queen	Chapel Royal, St James's Palace
Camping, Outdoor Life and Travel Association Exhibition	Olympia
Ceremony commemorating the execution of Charles I	Charing Cross and Banqueting Hall

February

Cruft's Dog Show	Olympia
English Folk Dance and Song Society's Festival	Royal Albert Hall
National Canoe Exhibition	Crystal Palace
Sir John Cass Service to commemorate the death of the City Sheriff who founded the school named after him in 1709. The pupils of the school wear red feather quills in their hats and lapels in memory of the blood-stained pen with which he drew up his will	St Botolph, Aldgate
Stampex: National Stamp Exhibition	New Horticultural Hall
The Trial of the Pyx. This is the occasion when the coins of the realm are tested. (It occasionally takes place in March.) The verdict is given in May	Goldsmith's Hall
Ideal Home Exhibition	Olympia

Pancake Race (Shrove Tuesday): occasionally	Soho
Stationers' Company Service (Ash Wednesday)	St Paul's Cathedral

March

National Cross Country Championships	Parliament Hill
St Bridewell Service is a service of dedication and thanksgiving for the foundation of the Royal Hospital, Bridewell. Attended by the Lord Mayor, the Sheriffs and the school children of King Edward VI School, Whitley	St Bride's, Fleet Street
London Dinghy Exhibition	Crystal Palace
Physics Exhibition	Alexandra Palace
Orange and Lemon Service when, after the special service, oranges and lemons are distributed to school children	St Clement Danes
Druids celebrate the Spring equinox	Tower Hill
Oxford v Cambridge Boat Race (sometimes takes place in April)	Putney-Mortlake (Thames)
Spital Service and Procession. Led by the Lord Mayor, the Aldermen and the Common Councilmen, a splendid procession attends a service at St Lawrence Jewry	Guildhall House-St Lawrence Jewry

Easter (Holy Week)

Tuesday: St Matthew Passion	St Paul's Cathedral
Maundy Thursday: Presentation of Maundy Money by the Queen to pensioners	Westminster Abbey (Occasionally held at other churches)
Good Friday: Butterworth Charity. A presentation of hot cross buns and money is made to poor widows after the 11.00 service when these gifts are laid out on tombstones	St Bartholomew the Great
Saturday: Fairs	Blackheath, Hampstead, Wormwood Scrubs
Covent Garden has a superb show of flowers on Easter Eve	
Sunday: Easter Parade	Battersea Park
Monday: Procession and Carols	Westminster Abbey
London Horse Harness Parade	Regent's Park
Fairs	Blackheath; Hampstead; Wormwood Scrubs

April
Greater London Festival (onwards)

John Stowe Commemoration Service. At this service the Lord Mayor presents a prize for the best essay on London by a London school child. The old quill pen held by the statue of Stowe is replaced by a new one.	St Andrew's Undershaft
Transportation Engineering Exhibition	Imperial College
Shakespeare's Birthday Service	Southwark Cathedral
Shakespeare Festival	Southwark
Primrose Day Ceremony	Parliament Square
Junior Fashion Fair	New Horticultural Hall
London Athletics Club—Schools Meeting	Crystal Palace

May

May Day: Labour Party procession	Hyde Park
Putney and Hammersmith Amateur Regattas	Putney and Hammersmith (Thames)
Royal Academy Summer Exhibition	Burlington House
Camden Arts Festival	Camden
Battersea Festival Gardens open	Battersea Park
Historic Commercial Vehicles London-Brighton run	Clapham (British Transport Museum)
Pepy's Commemoration Service	St Olave's, Hart Street
Trinity House Service	St Olave's, Hart Street
London-Brighton walk	Westminster Bridge
Oak-apple Day (Founder's Day)	Chelsea Royal Hospital
Commemoration of the death of Henry VI	Tower of London
Beating the Bounds (every 3 years)	Tower of London
Boat Afloat Show	Little Venice
Chelsea Flower Show	Chelsea Royal Hospital
London Private Fire Brigades Competition. On this occasion 66 brigades compete in target spraying. Bring raincoats and wellingtons. (This sometimes takes place in June.)	Guildhall Yard
Festival of London Stores. (Usually towards the end of June.)	

Whitsun

Church Parade	Tower of London

Spring Bank Holiday

Saturday and Monday: National Sheepdog trials	Hyde Park
Fairs	Blackheath; Hampstead; Wormwood Scrubs

June

Son et Lumière (until September)	St Paul's Cathedral
Trooping of the Colour. (Rehearsals are held on the two previous Saturdays. The first is free: the second costs 50p. Apply to the Brigade Major, Household Division, Horse Guards, Whitehall, SW1.)	Horse Guards—Buckingham Palace
Election of Sheriffs. This is an event that goes back to 1132 and in its present form to 1475	Common Hall, Guildhall
Presentation of the Knollys Rose to the Lord Mayor. This commemorates a quit-rent imposed in 1381 when the Lord Mayor built a bridge from the house of the wife of Sir Robert Knollys to a property across the road	Mansion House
Royal Tournament March Past	Battersea Park
Royal Tournament. (Occasionally early in July.)	Earl's Court

July

Signor Pasquali Favali's Marriage Portion. Marriage dowries are presented by the Corporation to three 'poor honest' young women aged 16-25 according to the bene-factor's wishes	Guildhall
Doggett's Coat and Badge Race, a sculling race on the Thames, is the oldest race in England, first competed for in 1716. The winner receives a splendid red coat and silver badge	London Bridge—Cadogan Pier
Swan-Upping on the Thames goes on over a period of several weeks. The Swan Masters and their assistants, all splendidly dressed, mark the swans on their beaks— the number of nicks mark ownership. A Swan Banquet is held periodically	Thames
Royal International Horse Show	Wembley
Beating the Bounds of the Liberty of the Savoy	Queen's Chapel of the Savoy
City of London Festival (Held every 2 years 1972, 1974, etc.)	City of London
Road Sweeping to the Vinters' Company follows the installation of the new Master. Porters in clean white smocks sweep a passage clean with besom brooms	Vintner's Hall to St James's Garlickhythe

for the members of the Court who carry
bouquets of sweet herbs

August

Cart Marking is carried out when the City Arms are marked on the shafts of carts plying for hire and numbers are placed on the shafts	Guildhall Yard
Cockpit Theatre and Arts Workshop (until September)	Cockpit Theatre
International Handicrafts and Do-It-Yourself Exhibition	Olympia

Summer Bank Holiday

Saturday and Monday: Greater London Horse show	Clapham Common
Fairs	Blackheath; Hampstead; Wormwood Scrubs

September

Horse of the Year Show	Wembley
Battle of Britain Day Fly Past	London
Christ's Hospital Boys' March. A service is held at the church at which the Lord Mayor, Sheriffs and Aldermen are present together with the 'Bluecoat' boys and girls from Hertford School. The procession headed by a band goes to the Mansion House where the Lord Mayor gives customary gifts.	Holy Sepulchre, Holborn
Admission of Sheriffs is the occasion when the Sheriffs-Elect and the Liverymen of their company go to the Guildhall—a really magnificent procession.	Guildhall
Election of the Lord Mayor is a ceremony called 'Common Hall'. There has been a Lord Mayor of London since 1192. This occasion is to select a new one	Guildhall

October

Opening of the Law Courts. This follows the annual breakfast of the Queen's Counsels, a service and a procession through the main hall of the Courts	St Margaret's, Westminster; Westminster Abbey; the Law Courts
Harvest-of-the-sea Thanksgiving is the occasion when the fishmerchants of Billingsgate decorate the church with fish and nets, and occasionally a boat	St Mary-at-Hill

Costermongers' Harvest Festival (Pearly Kings and Queens)	St Martin-in-the-Fields
Quits Rent Ceremony is the time when a billhook and hatchet are presented to the Queen's Remembrancer by the Controller and the City Solicitor instead of rents on two properties	Law Courts
International Dairy Show	Olympia
St Edward's Day Pilgrimage	Westminster Abbey
Lion Sermon is preached to commemorate the escape from a lion of a Lord Mayor, Sir John Gayor, when he was in Arabia	St Katherine Creechurch
Motor Show	Earl's Court
International Audio Festival and Fair	Olympia
Trafalgar Day Ceremony	Trafalgar Square
Horse of the Year Show	Earl's Court
Ladies' Kennel Association Championship Dog Show	Olympia

November

Admission Ceremony of Lord Mayor Elect is when the outgoing Lord Mayor hands over the City Insignia to his successor. No words are spoken at this time and has become known as 'the Silent Change'.	Guildhall
The Lord Mayor's Procession has taken place since 1215. Originally it was intended to show the citizens of London their new Lord Mayor as he went to swear his allegiance to the Sovereign. He now takes the oath at the Law Courts.	Guildhall-Strand
Veteran Car Run from London-Brighton	Hyde Park Corner
State opening of Parliament is a splendid occasion with a colourful procession as the Queen in the Irish State Coach drives from Buckingham Palace to the House of Lords	Buckingham Palace-House of Lords
International Cycle and Motor-Cycle Show	Earl's Court
Messiah	St Paul's Cathedral
St Cecilia Day Service and Festival	Holy Sepulchre, Holborn
Cross-Country Championships	Parliament Hill
Armistice Day Ceremony	Cenotaph
National Exhibition of Cage and Aviary Birds	Alexandra Palace

December

National Careers Exhibition	Olympia
Ernest Reed Christmas Concert	Royal Festival Hall
Judo Open Individual Championships	Crystal Palace
Richmond Championship Dog Show	Olympia
Royal Smithfield Show and Exhibition	Earl's Court
Carol Singing	Trafalgar Square
Church Parade	Tower of London
Grand Christmas Pudding Presentation—Australian gift to the Lord Mayor	Mansion House
Nativity Play	St Peter-upon-Cornhill
Christmas Eve (afternoon): Blessing the Crib	St Paul's Cathedral; Westminster Abbey
A Christmas Howyahooha for Kids	Queen Elizabeth Hall
National Cat Club Championship Show	Olympia

Adventure Playgrounds

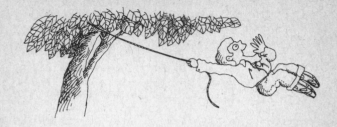

Have you ever wanted to light a fire in the middle of London, to build a house, or to swing, Tarzan-like, from tree to tree? Well, now you can. You can do all those things and a great deal more in Adventure Playgrounds.

A lot of people think that they cater mainly for small children and although 2 year-olds can and do use them, they play during the day leaving the field clear for older people after school. During the holidays and weekends everyone joins in but the smaller ones usually have their activities supervised by special nursery teachers or experienced play leaders.

Most playgrounds have an out-door area. This is a space where you can light those fires, build those tree-houses and use those tree-ropes. You can make your own camp with your friends or join in with other activities. There is usually a football pitch and space for other outdoor games as well.

In bad weather you can use the hut to paint or model, dress-up and act, or to take part in indoor games. The very young have things like plasticine and sand-pits provided for them while, in some Adventure Playgrounds, the older ones can dance or look at films. Occasionally outside trips, like going to a swimming-pool or the cinema are organised as an extra facility.

There are Adventure Playgrounds all over London but we have only listed a few of them. If you want to know if there is one in your area get in touch with the **London Adventure Playground Association** or the local borough surveyor's and engineer's department.

Ampton Adventure Playground, Ampton Street, Gray's Inn Road, WC1, Tel: 837 4536
This centre offers special provision for under 5s during weekdays. Extras include a football pitch, a sand play centre and, in the hut, leathercraft, painting and sewing.
Open: Monday-Friday 10.00-20.00; Saturday and Sunday 10.00-18.00.
Brandon Activities Playground, Lorrimore Square, SE17, Tel: 735 1312
This is especially good for those interested in art because painting, collages and crafts are all carried on in the hut.

15

Open: Tuesday-Friday 17.00-19.00 (under 5s 14.00-16.00); Saturday 10.00-16.00.

Christchurch Gardens, Commercial Street, E1, Tel: 638 8681

There is special provision for under 5s during weekdays in term time (10.00-12.00). Extras include a football pitch, sandpits and, in the hut, facilities for chess, table tennis and crafts. This centre also runs a discotheque.

Open: Monday-Friday 16.00-20.00 (in term time); 9.00-17.00 (in holidays) Saturday 9.00-16.00.

Cumberland Centre, Varndell Street, Hampstead Road, NW1, Tel: 387 0286

A trained nursery staff looks after under 5s from 10.00-12.30 and 13.30-15.30. This centre is unusual since it caters for people up to the age of 21. Special activities include camping, visits to the sea and to the theatre. It has its own discotheque as well.

Open: Monday-Friday 10.00-21.00 Saturday and Sunday 10.00-18.00.

Parkhill Adventure Playground, 29-31 Parkhill Road, NW3, Tel: 722 0331

This enormous area of three acres gives lots of opportunity to learn to camp, garden and build. It has two floodlit football pitches and in the hut, a chance to cook, do arts and crafts, play table tennis and so on.

Open: Monday-Friday 16.00-20.00 (term time); 10.00-20.00 (holidays); Saturday 10.00-18.30.

Sands End, Langford Road, SW6, Tel: 736 7065

Apart from the Adventure Playground this centre has a football pitch outside and table tennis indoors. There is a discotheque every Friday. Younger children can paint, draw and dress up.

Open: Tuesday-Friday 16.00-20.00 (term time); 10.00-20.00 (holidays); Saturday 10.00-18.00; Sunday 10.00-17.00.

Whitfield Gardens Centre, Whitfield Street, W1, Tel: 636 8514

The outside area has a climbing frame, a football pitch and room for other organised games like rounders. Inside the hut you can paint, draw, do crafts, learn to cook and play games.

Open: Monday-Friday 10.00-20.00.

(For other types of centres look under **One O'Clock Clubs, Playparks, Pre-School Playgroups, Theatre.**)

Animals and Birds

The London Zoo is not the only place in London where you will find animals and birds. Many parks and open spaces have their own small animal corners or sanctuaries. There are plenty of pet shops and there is even a street market for animals. Bird-watchers will find more to do than just feeding the pigeons in Trafalgar Square. There are animals in captivity, animals running wild, animals to ride and animals to feed— and if you are really keen on natural history you can join the XYZ Club.

The XYZ Club, the Young Zoologist's Club, is based on Regent's Park and Whipsnade Zoos. The club was started in 1959 and its activities have expanded over the years. Today it has over 4000 members, most of them living in or around London, although a few live as far away as Trinidad and Hongkong.

There are a lot of advantages attached to membership. When you join you receive a club badge, a membership card and six free tickets to Regent's Park Zoo and Whipsnade. The journal 'Zoo Magazine' is sent to you 3 times a year and the XYZ Information Bureau will answer any queries about natural history. During the holidays there are lectures, forums, brains trusts and film shows. There are animal collecting trips, field courses, demonstrations in animal photography and talks on animal care.

The Club is open to people of 9-18 and membership costs £1 a year but there is a reduced rate for schools and other groups. If you want to join you should write to the Secretary of the Club.

ZOOS

Regent's Park Zoo in the heart of London has a collection of over 7000 animals. The 'London Zoo Guide' which costs 15p is really good value for money because it not only provides information about the Zoo's inhabitants but it gives you a good map as well. It is impossible to list all the things to see but don't miss one of the newest animal houses, the 'Moonlight World' of the small mammal house. Day and night have been reversed so you can actually see nocturnal animals like bats and badgers going about their night-time activities.

The Snowdon Aviary, opened in 1965, is the Zoo's first out-door home for birds. You can walk inside and see herons, kestrels, ibises, spoonbills and other birds swooping around in comparative freedom.

There are, of course, animals like camels and Shetland ponies to ride. The famous Chimpanzees' Tea Party takes place on the lawn close to the Clock Tower, but if you want to have a really good look, get there early.

The Zoo enforces the rule about not feeding the animals very strictly but you will have plenty of opportunity to watch them being fed.
Battersea Park Children's Zoo which is open from Easter to September has become increasingly popular. It now includes exotic animals and birds from all over the world besides the domestic animals you can make a fuss of. It has otters, coatimundis, squirrels, chimpanzees, monkeys, donkeys and other animals. A new aviary has been built for birds like mynahs, tanagers and the magnificent cocks-of-the-rock. There are pony rides most of the day.

Admission to this Zoo is very cheap and it includes entrance to the funfair.
Crystal Palace Children's Zoo started life as a pets' corner in 1953 but since then it has grown enormously. The domestic animals are allowed to wander about while the other animals have attractive enclosures.

There is a penguin pond and birds like rheas, cranes and egrets in outside enclosures. This, too, is a place for pony rides.

Mobile Zoo is organised by the GLC since not everyone can manage to go to the main zoos. This one visits different parks during the school holidays. Each visit lasts 5 days and last year it went to 22 different parks. The exhibits come from Crystal Palace Zoo and are transported in horse boxes. The tame animals are put into small enclosures where they can be handled; a specially designed caravan houses the others like monkeys, cockatoos and chipmunks. Shetland and Welsh ponies are brought along for rides.

To find out if the zoo will be coming to one of your local parks, get in touch with the GLC Parks Department.

Zoos Outside London include Chessington, Whipsnade and Windsor Safari Park. These are all within easy reach of London and the fares are not impossible provided you use Red or Golden Rovers.

ANIMAL ENCLOSURES, AVIARIES AND SANCTUARIES

Many parks have aviaries and animal enclosures. Some of them are listed below:

Battersea Park: fallow deer, sheep, waterfowl.

Brockwell Park: quail, touracos, toucans, jays and other birds.

Clissold Park: crane, fallow and Chinese water deer, rabbits, peafowl, mynah birds, black-necked swan and other waterfowl.

Dulwich Park: quail, touracos, mots-mots, toucans and other exotic birds and waterfowl.

Golders Hill Park: fallow and Chinese deer, pygmy goats, sheep, rabbits, pheasants, peacocks and waterfowl.

Holland Park: peafowl, junglefowl, pheasants, geese and crane. On the north side there is a woodland with exotic plants and trees where these birds can best be seen.

Maryon Wilson Park: ponies, fallow and Chinese water deer and jacob sheep.

Regent's Park: chiff-chaff, flycatchers, redstarts, willow warblers, whitethroats and other birds are best seen in the sanctuary by the lake.

St James's Park: ducks, pelicans, flamingoes and many other birds. On the Mall side of the lake are information boards with named pictures of the birds to help you identify them.

Streatham Common: rookery open to the public.

Sydenham Wells Park: many splendid birds including flamingoes.

Victoria Park: fallow and Chinese water deer, bantams, guinea fowl, cranes, rabbits and many other birds and small animals.

Waterlow Park: jays, quail, touracos, black swans, geese, doves, mynah birds and other birds.

ANIMALS AND BIRDS IN THE WILD

All the parks and open spaces listed below have wild birds and small animals.

18

Barn Elms Reservoir: fantastic numbers of ducks and other waterfowl.
Epping Forest: deer, foxes, badgers, rabbits.
Hampstead Heath, Golders Hill Park, Kenwood: birds, hundreds of almost tame squirrels, and foxes.
Richmond Park, Bushey Park: deer roam freely here.
Walthamstow Reservoirs: a breeding ground for herons and the great crested crebe. You must get a permit from the Metropolitan Water Board before you go.

PET SHOPS
There are, of course, plenty of pet shops all over London besides those mentioned, as well as homes run by the animal protection societies where you can get a pet. Don't make the elementary mistake of buying one without your parents' permission, and don't even consider having a pet unless you know you can look after it properly—and that can mean hard work as well as giving up other things you might want to do.
Club Row is a market in the East End, open only on Sunday mornings. It is under the close supervision of the RSPCA and so if you are in doubt about the animal you are thinking of buying, look for the inspector.
Fitzgibbon Zoological Suppliers, 17 George Street, Romford, Essex is a shop specialising in exotic birds and animals.
Harrods Children's Zoo, Brompton Road, Knightsbridge, SW1, Tel: 730 1234 has a really good pets' department with usual and unusual animals and birds. If you happen to want an elephant, this is the place to order one from.
Palmer's, 35 Parkway, NW1, Tel: 485 5167 has unusual animals like giant South-American toads, tree-frogs and baby alligators.

OTHER PLACES TO VISIT
Battersea Dogs' Home is a refuge where lost dogs are taken and some-times claimed and visitors are welcome. The noise is indescribable since there are usually about 100 dogs in residence.
Battersea Park has a dolphinarium where you can be entertained for hours at a stretch.
London Dolphinarium has polished performances by these intelligent fish several times a day.
Royal Mews has marvellous horses, gleaming harness and magnificent coaches.
Don't forget the Changing of the Horse Guards. (See under **Daily Ceremonies.**)

MUSEUMS
Epping Forest Museum is particularly interested in conservation and has exhibits of the animal, bird and plant life in Epping Forest and man's association with it.
Natural History Museum has a special Children's Centre. It is open for those between 10-14 who are really keen on natural history. You have

to submit an entrance project before you are admitted but this isn't nearly as fearsome as it sounds. Ask any official at the museum about it.

Once you are a member you can attend films and talks, take part in the field trips organised about once a month and go on the planned tours which link different parts of the museum together. They have for instance, 'Wild Life in Danger' and 'Australian Tour'. Brochures are available and there is both the room and the opportunity for you to actually work there if you want to.

SHOWS AND EXHIBITIONS

Arab Horse Show; Cruft's Dog Show; Greater London Horse Show; Hammersmith Canine Society Show (Alexandra Palace); Horse of the Year Show; Ladies' Kennel Club Championship Dog Show; London Championship Show of Small Pets; London Horse Harness Parade; National Cat Club Championship Show; National Exhibition of Cage and Aviary Birds; Royal International Horse Show; Sheep-Dog Trials (Hyde Park); Swan-Upping on the Thames. (For further details see **Calendar.**)

STRAY ANIMALS

If you find a stray animal or bird, or one that is injured, take it to the RSPCA or the NSPCA who will look after it.

TRAINING OF DOGS

If you have a dog, see that it is properly trained. Ask you local council for the nearest dog training centre or get in touch with the Canine Defence League. You can get pamphlets on the care of animals from the RSPCA headquarters.

Arms and Armour

At odd times throughout the year, guns still thunder salutes in London.

Almost certainly it will be the Honourable Artillery Company and the King's Troop, Royal Horse Artillery at work.

On occasions such as the Queen's official birthday, the Honourable Artillery Company who have the right to march through the City of London with bayonets fixed, drums beating and colours flying, fire their guns from Tower Wharf.

The King's Troop, Royal Horse Artillery, famous for their musical rides, gallop into Hyde Park, gun carriages dragged behind magnificent horses, and fire the salutes from there.

However, if you simply want to look at arms and armour, there are plenty of places to go.

MUSEUMS

Bethnal Green Museum has a really fascinating collection of Japanese Samurai armour.

British Museum has a large collection, but make a point of examining the Assyrian armour and weapons.

Imperial War Museum has a comprehensive collection from 1914 onwards. This includes vehicles, uniforms, weapons, plans, maps, artists' impressions of campaigns, and aircraft.

London Museum has an interesting collection. This museum is particularly good on the Civil War period.

National Army Museum is London's newest museum. It has material up to the outbreak of the 1914-18 war, its final exhibit being the orders for mobilisation in 1914.

Rotunda Artillery Museum has a superb collection of guns and muskets.

Royal Small Arms Factory has a fantastic collection of small arms, bayonets and automatic weapons in the Pattern Room.

Tower of London, once a fortress, a prison and a menagerie as well as being a royal residence, now contains the largest collection of early arms and armour in Britain. There are a number of rooms and they are all packed with exhibits. Look out for Henry VIII's armour and his walking stick—a spiked club with three pistol-barrels. There is Charles I's gilt armour and that belonging to Robert Dudley, Earl of Essex and favourite of Elizabeth I.

Victoria and Albert Museum has highly ornamented European armour as well as a lot of examples of Oriental work.

Wallace Collection has good examples of armour and weapons, much of it Oriental.

Westminster Abbey, curiously enough, has a number of things worth looking at in the Abbey Museum. There is, for instance, the sword that Henry V used at Agincourt, and the effigy of General Monk in full armour.

SHOPS

Although there are a number of shops specialising in arms and armour, these tend to be fairly expensive. If you are just hoping to start a collection you should wander through the markets. The Portobello Road, for example, has a number of specialist stalls where you can have a good look round and talk to some knowledgeable people about them.

Art and Craft

This is a section on **doing** art. It concentrates on the centres which have facilities available and the shops which stock things you might need. Besides the places mentioned, most youth centres, adventure playgrounds and playparks usually have a room and materials for you to use and, in some cases, qualified people to help you. Pottery, brass rubbing, puppetry, and needlework have sections of their own. In the section on theatre you will find yet more places where you can do arts and crafts specifically connected with the theatre.

CLUBS AND CENTRES

Arts Study Centre is open in the holidays and while you can concentrate on the things you like, the idea is show how they can link up together. You can paint, model and print from 9.30-12.30, and keep it up during term time on Saturday mornings. There are 5 groups splitting the age range which is from 4-14.

Bethnal Green Museum has a room on Saturdays from 11.00-12.30 and 14.00-16.00 where people of all ages are able to paint, draw, weave, model with plasticine and so on. This museum has many examples of craftwork and you can link up what you are doing with what is on show.

Camden Arts Centre is open on Saturdays and Sundays for people of 6-16. This is a place where you are actually taught and the lessons include painting, construction, pottery and etching. You must book for a whole year—that is, 3 terms of 10 weeks each. The lessons tend to be rather expensive but the tuition is of a tremendously high standard.

Children's Theatre Workshop meets on Saturday from 9.30-12.30 and apart from opportunities to do arts and craft you can help with the plays that actually get performed in public.

Cockpit Theatre and Arts Workshop is a really super centre where you can do design and graphics among other things and there is another workshop for crafts connected with the theatre. In the foyer is free exhibition space for paintings, sculpture and photographs.

Craft Workshop is the place to go if you are over 10 and want to learn enamelling. This centre organises weekend courses lasting about 6 hours on each of the 2 days. The all-in price is £4.25.

Geffrye Museum has a centre open on Saturdays and during the school holidays for anyone who wants to take part in practical activities. Some of them, based on the exhibits in the museum, involve drawing, cutting-out, assembling information, colouring and working out puzzles and using games. There are also art and craft activities including modelling, pottery, puppetry and model-making going on at the same time. The morning sessions are for 7-10 year olds, the afternoon ones for people over 11. Although this is run mainly for local people, visitors are welcome to join in whenever there is room for them.

The Glasshouse is a place where you can go and watch glass-blowing. There are classes for older children but they are quite expensive. A 3-week course costs about £20 but you do get super teachers.

Horniman Museum Children's Centre is open to anyone between the ages of 9-16 who can get there fairly frequently. The aim is to use the exhibits in the museum as a starting point for drawing, painting and craft work. The activities include modelling, pottery, embroidery, toy-making and lino-block printing.

Everything in the centre is free and there is a long waiting list for membership. To qualify you have to make 3 attendances at the museum to draw or study some of the exhibits because they want people who are really interested. Anyone who does not belong to the Club can still borrow drawing materials from the children's room if they need them.

Inter-Action has a section of its own but it is worth mentioning now that it organises Drama-Scapes where all sorts of arts and crafts take place, centred round one theme. Previously these have included Dinosaurs, Moby Dick, and Gulliver and the Lilliputians. There is a small craft workshop as well and, for under 7s, there are creative play activities.

Lamble Centre is a workshop for people up to the age of 11. The activities include painting, fabric printing, drama, music, woodwork, cooking and model-making. It is open from 9.00-16.00 for parents with under 5s, and from 16.00-19.00 for anyone up to the age of 11.

Moonrock is, for the moment, at the Free School, Regent's Park Road although there is a possibility it might be moving. It is open all day on Saturdays from 11.00 and admittance is 10p. Activities include music, painting, various kinds of crafts, stories and films, all taking place in an informal atmosphere.

Theatre Centre is a place where you can do pottery, sculpture and painting as well as any other craft connected with the theatre or the cinema. It is open every Wednesday from 16.30-18.00 for anyone from 9-11, and from 19.00-21.00 for people between 11-13. It is free for your first visit so that you have a chance to find out if it is your sort of place. The price is then 5p a time.

Victoria and Albert Museum always has a number of activities going on on Saturdays. There are lectures, projects and opportunities to draw and paint. A member of the museum staff is around if you want some help. It is open for people of 7-10 from 10.15-11.45, and for 11-15s from 15.00-15.45. The holiday programmes are so varied and interesting that you'll find it well worth getting in touch with them.

SHOPS

Alec Tiranti Ltd, 72 Charlotte Street, W1, Tel: 636 8565 have materials for carving, pottery, moulding and enamelling.

Candle-makers Supplies, 387 King Street, W6, Tel: 748 8896 have everything you are likely to need for this craft. They offer a free booklet and have a permanent exhibition.

Chelsea Art Stores, 314 Kings Road, SW3, Tel: 352 0430 has materials for painting and drawing.

Craftorama, 49 Shelton Street, WC2, Tel: 240 2745 is particularly good for people interested in lapidary.

Crafts Unlimited, 21 Macklin Street, WC2, Tel: 242 7053 have books, catalogues, equipment and materials for almost every craft you can think of including batik, cane and raffia, fabric printing and dyeing, jewellery and enamelling.

Eaton's, 16 Manette Street, W1, Tel: 937 9391 sell cane and raffia for basketwork and lampshades, together with a wonderful collection of shells, minerals and semi-precious stones.

Ells and Farrier, 5 Princes Street, W1, Tel: 629 9964 sell all kinds of beads, sequins and imitation stones.

Hobby Horse, 387 King Street, W6, Tel: 748 8896 has a good supply of all craft materials.

Kettle's, 127 High Holborn, WC1, Tel: 405 9764 has a marvellous supply of paper and boxes.

Langford and Hill, 9 Warwick Street, W1, Tel: 437 0086 has all graphic arts materials, colour aid and craft colour.

Letraset, 44 Gerrard Street, W1, Tel: 937 3242 is a pleasant shop where you can buy all their lettering and graphic arts products.

Paper Chase, 216 Tottenham Court Road, W1, Tel: 637 1121 has a fantastic selection of paper of all kinds.

Reeves', 13 Charing Cross Road, WC2, Tel: 930 9940, 178 Kensington High Street, W8, Tel: 937 5370 sell their own paints and artists' materials.

Rowney's, 12 Percy Street, W1, Tel: 636 8241 have their own paints and artists' materials.

Spectrum, 37 Church Road, Wimbledon, Tel: 946 2930 sell everything you are likely to need for painting and drawing.

LOOKING AT CRAFTS

Craft Centre of Great Britain is a centre with examples of young artists' work. Occasionally the artists themselves are around for you to talk to.
Crafts Council Gallery has a permanent but constantly changing exhibition of crafts, and an information centre. On display and for sale are pottery, textiles, woodwork, cane and rushwork, glassware, metalwork, jewellery, calligraphy, silverware and musical instruments.
The Glasshouse see above.

Art Galleries and Exhibitions

There are art galleries all over London, many of them having special exhibitions besides still keeping their permanent collections on show. Probably the best thing to do is to get the 'Art Gallery Guide' which is published monthly by the **Arts Exhibition Bureau.** You can have a regular monthly subscription of up to 3 copies sent by post for only 50p.

Although at the moment most art galleries are free, special exhibitions usually cost between 15-30p. (Twice as much for adults, of course.) Small exhibitions in picture-dealers' shops are normally free and so are the open-air exhibitions.

A quick list of the galleries is given below:
Courtauld Institute Galleries has the superb Courtauld Collection of Impressionists and post-Impressionists and the Roger Fry Collection.
Dulwich College Picture Gallery was London's first public art gallery. Designed by Sir John Soane in 1814, it has Gainsboroughs, Rembrandts, and Van Dyck's and examples of many other notable artists.
Guildhall Art Gallery has, naturally enough, a really fascinating collection of pictures of London. Occasionally exhibitions of the work of London Art Societies are held there.
Hayward Gallery is part of the new South Bank Arts Centre. It is meant for temporary exhibitions of the Arts Council and as well as the two-level galleries, there are three open-air sculpture courts.
Iveagh Bequest, Kenwood, is a collection of works presented by Lord

Iveagh and containing works by Cuyp, Rembrandt, Romney, Reynolds, and Vermeer and others. It is a small collection in a friendly setting so its a good place to begin looking at pictures if you've never done it before.

Leighton House Art Gallery is an extraordinary house containing a collection of High Victorian art including works by Burne-Jones, Millais, Stevens and Watts besides that of Lord Leighton himself. People under 16 must be accompanied by an adult.

National Gallery, rudely christened the National Cruet Stand when it was built in 1838, has one of the world's great collections. Don't even try to see everything in one go or you'll come away confused and exhausted. A good way of getting to know about pictures is to go to the lunch-time lectures. Pavement artists outside provide light relief.

National Portrait Gallery is a marvellous place. Famous artists have always painted both the famous and the infamous and here is a magnificent collection of faces to look at. The subject is more important than the artist but many of the most well-known names are represented here. In one room are portraits of our present royal family.

Queen's Gallery is actually a small gallery in Buckingham Palace containing a frequently changing exhibition of about 30 paintings from the Queen's famous collections, as well as furniture and small drawings.

Royal Academy of Arts is, perhaps, best known for its Summer Exhibition. This has been held every year since 1769 and means a great step forward for those young artists lucky enough to be chosen. During the winter there are often exhibitions of work lent by other collections.

Serpentine Gallery also holds a summer exhibition, but it is very different from the one at the Royal Academy. It shows the most modern of artists and their work and is entertaining to visit.

South London Art Gallery in Southwark has a fairly small collection of contemporary British paintings, watercolours and topographical drawings as well as a reference collection of 20th century prints.

Tate Gallery has three main sections: British art, modern sculpture and modern foreign paintings. There is a marvellous collection of Turners, many paintings by Blake, and a world-famous collection of Impressionists, as well as superb sculpture with many of the great names like Epstein, Picasso, Rodin and Moore well represented.

It holds special children's lectures in the holidays and these, far from being dull, are really good. There are free public lectures during the week too. It's worth a visit at tea-time. The restaurant has murals by Rex Whistler—and the tea and cakes are excellent.

Wallace Collection is housed in Hertford House which was built for the Duke of Manchester in 1776. Lady Wallace presented this absorbing collection which includes work by artists such as Valasquez, Watteau and Holbein, to the nation in 1897.

Whitechapel Art Gallery is a popular gallery for exhibitions of modern art, architecture and design and, since it has no permanent collection of its own, often borrows from the national galleries to put on excellent shows.

26

William Morris Gallery at Water House was the boyhood home of this Victorian poet, artist and socialist. It now contains an interesting collection of original designs of William Morris himself and of other artists of the same era.

OPEN AIR EXHIBITIONS

On Sundays you can see pictures exhibited for sale by the artists on the Green Park side of Piccadilly and on the Bayswater side of Hyde Park and Kensington Gardens. In Hampstead there is a lively exhibition in the summer months. In May and June there is one in Victoria Embankment Gardens and one is being organised in South End Green in Hampstead. The works vary from the really awful, through the competent but dull, to really interesting and accomplished work.

On Thursday and Friday each week there is an art market in Camden Passage. The artists are there at work so you can go and watch them.

As well as all this, there are exhibitions of sculpture in the open air at Battersea and Holland Parks. These might well range from one-man shows to international exhibitions.

Athletics

Most people have some idea of whether they are good or hopeless at athletics but many others, although they enjoy them, don't seem to realise that although they will never be first class they are equally important. How can there be competition without competitors? If you are at all interested, go along to one of the centres or tracks. You will be welcomed and might well find that an event you hadn't even thought of is the right one for you.

The **Central Council of Physical Recreation** is very helpful and knows exactly what is going on where and how you can best take part.

The new **Crystal Palace National Sports Centre** has marvellous facilities. The best way to join is to become an Authorised User. This costs 50p for the year or if the whole family joins then it is a lot cheaper. After that, whenever you use the track, gym or pool, you pay a small sum each time. If you are within reach of the Crystal Palace and are interested in almost any sport, this is the place to go.

Other centres are at Battersea Park, Dulwich Park, Finsbury Park, Herne Hill, King George's Fields, Stepney, Parliament Hill, Wormwood Scrubs and Victoria Park.

The **Ladywell Centre** has very cheap classes in gymnastics for people of all ages. Membership is 25p a year and each visit is 3p unless you are under 5 when it is free. It is open for under 5s on Monday, Tuesday and Thursday from 15.00-16.00; girls aged from 5-9 on Monday and Wednesday from 16.30-17.15; girls aged 10-15 on Monday and Wednesday from 17.15-18.15; boys in similar ages groups at similar times on Tuesday and Thursday. It is open for over 15s in the evening when there are athletics, trampoline, badminton, table tennis and basketball.

Many Youth Centres run classes in the evening with first class coaches around.

If you want to know what is going on in athletics get the 'Amateur Athletics Association' diary. All the major events in London are held at either the **Crystal Palace** or the **White City**.

ARCHERY

There are a surprising number of clubs with their own grounds in London. On the whole they tend to be expensive because each person taking part has to be insured. The **British Field Archery Association** is the body to approach for information.

The other way of taking part in this increasingly popular sport is to go along to the Crystal Palace (see under **Athletics**).

Boats and Boating

Since the earliest settlements in London were by the side of the Thames, it is not surprising that a lot of the things to do and see are connected with the river.

There is a great deal of archaeological evidence for this. The museums hold lots of exhibits like swords, both Roman and Viking, pottery, brooches and coins that have been discovered close by. Even today some people regularly search the mud flats, sometimes making surprising discoveries.

The Thames, of course, has always been used for transport, and although the days are gone when it was so crowded that it was said that people could cross from one side to the other without getting their feet wet, it is still possible to take river trips and get a different view of London.

BOAT TRIPS (Thames)

Boat trips are organised from April to September. Check times by ringing Charing Cross. Tower or Westminster Pier.

Charing Cross Pier-Greenwich: launches leave at 45-60 minute intervals on a trip taking 50 minutes each way from 10.30-17.00 daily.

Charing Cross Pier-Tower of London: launches leave at 30 minute intervals on a trip taking 30 minutes each way from 10.00-17.00 daily.

Tower Pier-Greenwich: launches leave at 30 minute intervals on a trip taking 30 minutes each way from 10.00-17.00 daily.

Westminster Pier-Battersea Pier: launches leave at 20 minute intervals on a trip taking 20 minutes each way from 10.00-dusk.

Westminster Pier Circular Trip (Lambeth-Greenwich) takes approximately 2 hours.

Westminster Pier-Greenwich: launches leave at 20 minute intervals on a trip taking 50 minutes each way from 10.20-dusk.

Westminster Pier-Hampton Court (Putney-Kew-Richmond-Kingston-Hampton Court): launches leave at 30 minute intervals on a trip taking 4 hours each way from 11.00-12.30 and 14.30-16.00 daily.

CANAL TRIPS

Jason's Trip: A 1½ hour barge trip along Regent's Canal, starting from the Canaletto Gallery opposite 60 Blomfield Road, W.9. Jason cruises to Hampstead Road Locks via Little Venice, a tunnel under Edgware Road, Regent's Park and the Zoo. A commentary is given on the return journey. The fare is 12½p for children with an adult, full fare 25p. Starting times vary according to the time of year, but usually they begin at 14.00 and 15.30 from April to September. Ring for full details and bookings.

On Saturday evenings there is a 4 hour cruise to Greenford in Middlesex along the Grand Union Canal leaving at 18.00 and costing 50p. On Friday evenings from July to September a barge leaves at 19.00 and covers the Regent's and Grand Union Canals to Camden Town and Harlesden. The fare for this is 50p. Jason is also available for private hire, school trips and children's birthday parties.

Jenny Wren: This is a narrow boat trip which starts at Camden High Street and takes you along Regent's Canal, through Camden Town Lock, the Zoo, Regent's Park, and then via the canal tunnel to Maida Vale, around the island at Little Venice, and return. The journey costs 15p (30p for adults) and takes 1½ hours. A commentary is given. Ring for details of times and special trips.

Zoo Water Bus The British Waterways Board's barge leaves from the Maida Vale end of Blomfield Road on 30 minute trips to the Zoo in

Regent's Park from Easter to September. It leaves on the hour Monday-Saturday from 10.00, and on Sundays from 14.00. The fare includes the price of entry to the Zoo. Last barge back from the Zoo leaves at 17.45.

OTHER BOAT TRIPS
This is not quite in the same category but you really can use the Woolwich Free Ferry which was opened in 1889, for free.

BOATS TO SEE
HMS Belfast, the last surviving great cruiser, moored opposite the Tower of London, has been turned into a permanent Royal Navy Museum. There is a great deal to see and there are films and records of actions at sea.

Cutty Sark, one of the most famous tea clippers, is permanently moored at Greenwich where her graceful lines dominate the waterfront. She has been refitted and rigged (her complete sailspread would cover three-quarters of an acre) as she was during her seagoing career. Down below is the 'Long John Silver' collection of curious and fascinating figure-heads, as well as an exhibition telling her history.

HMS Discovery, is the ship in which Captain Scott sailed on one of his voyages to the Antarctic. Inside are many of his personal possessions together with those of his companions. There are guided tours over the ship from 13.00-16.30.

Gipsy Moth IV is the famous boat in which Sir Francis Chichester sailed around the world in 1966. She is now moored next to the Cutty Sark at Greenwich.

BOAT CLUBS AND CENTRES (see also **Canoeing and Sailing**)
Cutty Sark Society is basically for those who are interested in nautical history.

Islington Boat Club is a club intended primarily for Islington residents although it does allow others to join. It is open on Tuesday and Wednesday from 17.00-19.00 and during the weekends with extensions during the Easter and summer holidays. You must be able to swim at least fifty yards before you can join.

Sea Cadets offer great opportunities for those interested in boats in return for naval-type training.

The Thames Barge Sailing Club is interested in the preservation, restoration and use of sailing barges.

MUSEUM
National Maritime Museum is really superb and gives a complete survey of British naval history. It has Nelson's relics, figure-heads, ship models, thousands of drawings, photographs and paintings, collections of uniforms, barges of various dignitaries, weapons and hundreds of other exhibits.

The New Neptune Hall has recently been opened. This shows the development and history of ships since the earliest times. There is a paddle tug in the centre and you can visit the crew's quarters and the engine room. Free film shows are given on Saturdays at 14.30 throughout the holidays.

EVENTS
Boat Afloat Show (see **Calendar**); Canoe race from Devizes to Westminster Bridge takes place at Easter; Doggett's Coat and Badge Race (see **Calendar**); Head of the River Race with up to 200 competing crews takes place from Mortlake-Putney usually on the same day as the Boat Race; National Boat Show (see **Calendar**); Putney, Hammersmith and Serpentine Amateur Regattas (see **Calendar**); Oxford and Cambridge Boat Race (see **Calendar**); Schools Head of the River Race is usually held in March or April. Wingfield Sculls, the major event for solo rowers, follows the Putney-Mortlake Course and usually takes place in May.

BOATS FOR HIRE
There are boats for hire at a reasonable price at Alexandra Palace Park, Battersea Park, Crystal Palace, Dulwich Park, Finsbury Park, Hyde Park, Regent's Park and Victoria Park. If you happen to want to go at the weekend or during the holidays, then get there early. Enormous queues form as the day warms up.

Books
There are plenty of bookshops in London. Charing Cross Road is the centre of the book trade and there are dozens of places where you can buy new or second-hand books or just browse.

Of course, the London libraries really are excellent. Most of them have children's sections and although it just isn't possible to name them all, the Buckingham Palace Road, Barnet, Holborn, Kensington, Lambeth and Swiss Cottage libraries are among the best. Most librarians are amazingly helpful and patient and a great number of them organise really good activities in the holidays and at weekends.

The London Borough of Barnet, for example, have a Children's Club for 9-12s with art work, craft, acting, discussions and story-telling going on, while Lambeth have story-tellers in the parks and playgrounds and send books around in vans.

The Foundation of Children's Book Groups is intended to further the interest of both parents and children in reading. There are interesting meetings, occasionally with authors talking, and sales of secondhand books are organised. The London 'Member at Large' is Ann Masnick, 34 Lincoln Avenue, SW19, Tel: 946 0409.

BOOK SHOPS

Bookshop 85, 85 Regents Park Road, NW1, Tel: 586 0512, has a good children's section with paperbacks only.

Book One, 23 Temple Fortune Parade, NW11, Tel: 458 1234, is an extremely good, alive place with a first-rate range of books. They sell only books for children and although there is someone to help you if you want it, there is never any pressure to make you hurry. There are regular Puffin Club meetings, schemes to help you choose, authors around and other activities, especially in the school holidays. It is the kind of place where you never know what might happen next, but whatever it is, you'll enjoy it.

Children's Book Centre, 140 Kensington Church Street, W8, Tel: 229 9646 is entirely devoted to children's books. It has a superb range of books and they produce a Children's Book Newsletter free 4 times a year. You should ask to be put on their mailing list for this. They also produce 'Reading for Enjoyment' at 15p for different age groups. An enormous number of activities go on here. There are reading hours every Wednesday at 16.30 except in November and December, occasional films, demonstrations and visits from authors.

Domino Bookshop, 3 Village Way, Beckenham, Kent, Tel 650 7799 is one of the best bookshops in South London and always carries a really good range for you to choose from. A really helpful staff will lend a hand if you want it, otherwise they leave you alone.

Foyles, 119 Charing Cross Road, WC2, Tel: 937 5660, is absolutely packed with books. They have a good children's department, sell second-hand books and run a children's book club.

Harrods, Brompton Road, Knightsbridge, SW1, Tel: 730 1234, has a carefully selected and very large area of space devoted to children's books and a helpful knowledgeable staff.

OLD BOOKS AND PRINTS

The collecting of old books and prints has become increasingly popular. You probably know of good local shops and there are dozens of them all over London. The markets are good hunting grounds. You should try the Antique Bazaar in Kensington, Chelsea Antique Market, Farringdon Road and the Portobello Road. You probably won't find any bargains but at least you will be charged a fair price.

MUSEUMS

British Museum has an unrivalled collection of printed books and manuscripts. Every publisher is legally bound to deposit a copy of every book, newspaper, pamphlet and periodical produced. The Newspaper Library is kept at Colindale.

The Manuscript Room has a superb collection of illuminated manuscripts from the 9th-16th centuries, two of the original copies of the Magna Carta, the log-book from the 'Victory', Captain Scott's diary, and the original of 'Alice in Wonderland' in its vast collection. In the

King's Library is the Gutenberg Bible, the first printed edition of Chaucer and Shakespeare and Caxton's original printing. (Caxton is buried in the churchyard of St Margaret's, Westminster.) There are letters and documents written by people like Cromwell, Nelson, Wellington, General Gordon and Mary, Queen of Scots.

The one place you won't be able to get into is the famous, domed library where a great number of people sit working at the same desks for years on end.

Chelsea Old Church has chained books, given to it by Sir Hans Sloane.

Dicken's House is where he lived with his family from 1837-9. It has a marvellous library of books by and about this great author, manuscripts, first editions, personal relics and, in the basement, the 'Dingley Dell' kitchen.

Keat's House was the home of John Keats, the poet who died young. It is here, in this really beautiful house in Hampstead, that he wrote his 'Ode to a Nightingale'. The house contains his manuscripts and letters.

London Museum has a really marvellous collection of documents and books, many of them about the London theatre, others relating to the London of Cromwellian times.

Public Records Office holds some of the most valuable national records of this country. The Domesday Book is kept here, together with Shakespeare's will, 17th century letters warning Lord Monteagle of the Gunpowder Plot, Wellington's despatch from the Battle of Waterloo, and the signatures of many people such as the kings and queens of England.

St Bride Printing Library has an absolutely fascinating collection of early printing machinery as well as many interesting books.

Science Museum has typesetting machinery which moves so slowly that you can actually see how it works.

Victoria and Albert Museum has an interesting collection of books showing the development of printing. The Print Room has leaves and cuttings of really beautifully illustrated medieval and renaissance manuscripts on display. Here you can see Dickens' manuscript of a 'Tale of Two Cities' and his desk.

Westminster Abbey has the 'Liber Regalis', the book that is used at every coronation. Printed in red and black, it is beautifully illustrated. The Library and Muniment Room which may only be visited by special permission has a truly fascinating collection of documents.

William Morris Gallery houses William Morris's own printing press and a collection of some of the books which were printed on it.

SHOWS AND EXHIBITIONS

Children's Book Show is the occasion on which publishers exhibit their new books. Originally it was always held in London in November. However, in 1971 it was held outside London for the first time, in Leeds. It now seems probable that there will be two book shows, one in London and one in the north. If you want to go, you should look in newspapers or ask at your local library. As well as the hundreds of books to look at, there are all sorts of other activities like visiting authors to speak to, quizzes and film shows.

The **National Book League** holds interesting exhibitions and shows throughout the year. The Antiquarian Booksellers' Association holds a Book Collectors' Fair there every June.

Brass Rubbing

The only shop in London where you can buy materials for brass rubbing is **Philips and Page Ltd**, 50 Kensington Church Street, London, W8, Tel: 937 5829.

They stock three qualities of paper and colour sticks in brown, bronze, black, gold, red, silver and red. You can also buy booklets about the technique of brass rubbing and get a list of the best places to go. Not all churches are willing to have people working in them and some require a small fee, so the list is invaluable.

The **London Museum** is anxious to acquire as many rubbings as possible of coal-hole covers. These iron plates, set into the pavements of London streets, are fast disappearing and the museum hopes that the public will help to record them. So, if you would like to have your rubbings preserved for posterity in the archives, send them in with your own name and address and the address of the street where you found them.

Bridges and Tunnels

We are so used to crossing the Thames that we hardly ever think about it, and if we do it is only to grumble that the bridge or the tunnel isn't exactly where we want it.

In fact, there was only one bridge across the Thames up to 1739— and that was London Bridge. Water traffic was important and hardly a bridge or tunnel was started without loud complaints by the watermen and lightermen that their livings were being taken away from them. Take the trouble to look at the bridges and to go down the tunnels. They are all different—many hideous, some beautiful.

Albert Bridge is a cantilever and suspension bridge, built in 1873 and named after Prince Albert, of course. Nearby is the figure of Atlanta.

Barnes Railway Bridge, constructed of iron, and opened in 1849, is hardly memorable but not objectionable.

Battersea Bridge, opened in 1890, and constructed of iron, replaced a wooden bridge frequently painted by Whistler. It is considered by almost everyone to be one of the ugliest in London.

Battersea Railway Bridge, opened in 1863, is the only railway bridge not connected to a main line terminus.

Blackfriars Bridge, built in 1899, was named after the priory of black-habited Dominican friars that backed onto the Thames. There is an underpass beneath the approach to the bridge and it was there that part of the hull of a Roman boat, now in the Guildhall Museum, was discovered.

Blackfriars Railway Bridge, a high iron structure, was built in 1886. To get a good view of it, stand on the road bridge and look across at it. There are interesting coats of arms at either end.

Blackwall Tunnel was a major engineering feat. It took 8 years to complete and was finally opened in 1897 for motor transport between Poplar and Greenwich. Since then, in 1967, a new twin tunnel has been constructed.

Cannon Street Railway Bridge was built in 1866 as part of the railway construction. On one side of the bridge, a train shed sticks out, adding to the general air of depression.

Chelsea Bridge is a suspension bridge, built in 1937, to replace an earlier one which had been there since 1858.

Chiswick Bridge, built in 1933, has the longest concrete arch of all the Thames bridges, stretching 150 feet.

Dartford Toll Tunnel, although planned as far back as 150 years, was not opened until 1967. It is for vehicles only and is a toll tunnel connecting Purfleet and Dartford.

Fulham Railway Bridge is a trellis girder bridge, built in 1889, with a footbridge running parallel to it.

Greenwich Foot Tunnel connecting Greenwich with the Isle of Dogs, is almost unexpected. On the Greenwich side the entrance, covered by a red brick dome with a cupola, is in Cutty Sark Gardens. In order to reach it, you have to descend by lift. The other end comes out in Island Gardens. You are sternly warned by a notice not to take down '... cattle or any animal forming part of a menagerie ...'

Hammersmith Bridge looking quite grand, perhaps because it incorporates the lower part of towers of an earlier bridge together with the abutments, has gilt iron pylons and is a suspension bridge. It was built in 1887 and quite a lot of people are fond of it—perhaps because of its associations with the Boat Race or because of the lovely view of the 18th century houses along the Mall.

Hungerford Bridge, the main railway bridge from Charing Cross, is probably London's ugliest bridge. The footbridge running alongside it does, however, give a magnificent view of the Thames.

Kew Bridge, built of stone and opened in 1903, is actually called Edward VII Bridge.

Kew Railway Bridge is a quite pleasant lattice girder bridge, built in 1869.

Lambeth Bridge, made of steel and opened in 1932, replaced an iron suspension bridge which had, in its turn, superseded the original horse ferry.

London Bridge, the original bridge of the nursery rhyme, was started in 1176, but not finished until 1209. The houses, shops and chapel of St Thomas à Becket that lined it paid rents which were supposed to help with its upkeep. It was on this bridge that the head of executed traitors were exhibited, stuck on spikes above the gatehouse to the drawbridge. In those days the Thames frequently froze and it was then that the Frost Fairs on the ice were held.

In 1831, the old bridge was replaced by a new one, made of granite, with five arches spanning the Thames. But as traffic has grown heavier each year and since it proved impossible to widen the bridge, it was decided to demolish it and build a new one.

This has been done very cleverly since the new one has been constructed round the old so that neither road nor river traffic has been interrupted. The old bridge has been transported, stone by stone, across the Atlantic to the United States of America.

Putney Bridge was built in 1884 to replace the old wooden toll bridge which was considered unsafe.

Richmond Bridge, constructed of stone, with five graceful arches and a parapet, was a toll bridge when it was built in 1777. It was successfully widened just before the Second World War.

Richmond Footbridge, built in 1894, is fascinating since there are three weir gates beneath the arches. They form a lock when lowered, making a barrier across the Thames.

Richmond Railway Bridge, made of iron and concrete, was built in 1848. Some people consider it a good example of railway bridge construction.

Rotherhithe Tunnel has alongside it an earlier one which was started in the 1800s. It was almost completed when, in 1808, it suddenly collapsed. The present tunnel which connects Stepney and Rotherhithe was opened in 1908 and is used by both vehicles and pedestrians. The circular air vents can be seen on either side of the Thames.

Southwark Bridge, opened in 1919, replaces an iron bridge which was built in the early 19th century.

Thames Tunnel, officially the Wapping-Rotherhithe Tunnel, was cut by Sir Marc Isambard Brunel. Although meant to be used as a road tunnel, it is now used by London Transport trains. It was opened in 1843 and took 11 years to complete although twice it had to be abandoned when the Thames broke through. Brunel gave a banquet in it in 1827 to celebrate the reopening of the project. It is possible to see the old shaft in Brunel Road. Perhaps the most interesting thing is not the tunnel itself but Brunel's tenacity. It was the first one to be constructed beneath the Thames and most people thought it impossible.

Tower Bridge, built in 1894, is quite unmistakable with its Gothic towers at either end, the bascules which operate and lift to allow ships to pass through. The towers house the hydraulic machinery and are the entrance to the lattice footbridge at the very top. (This is now closed to pedestrians.)

When a ship shows lights and flies a pennant to indicate that it wants to pass, the traffic lights turn red and a warning bell rings. In 1952 a bus was caught on the bridge as the two halves began to lift. Only the quick reaction of the driver saved it. He put his foot down on the accelerator and jumped the gap.

Tower Subway was meant as a subway for passenger traffic to Bermondsey and was opened in 1845. There was a 60 foot shaft and stationary engines pulled the carriages along, rather like a cable car. The top of the shaft can still be seen on Tower Hill. The tunnel is now used only to carry service pipes.

Twickenham Bridge is a wide, pleasant concrete bridge built in 1933.

Vauxhall Bridge is not particularly interesting. It was built in 1900 to replace an old iron bridge.

Victoria Railway Bridge, at 900 feet long and 132 feet wide was, when it was built in 1895, the widest in the world. Since then it has been widened again.

Waterloo Bridge, opened in 1937, is considered by many people to be the most graceful bridge over the Thames. It is made of beautiful smooth steel and concrete with five arches, each 240 feet wide.

Westminster Bridge, built in 1862, and made of cast-iron, offers a really superb view of the Thames. On one corner of it, you can see a statue of Queen Boadicea.

Woolwich Tunnel, which connects North Woolwich and Woolwich, was opened in 1912. It was only constructed because of the interruptions and delays in the Woolwich Free Ferry service.

Camping

Whether you are a Londoner trying to escape or someone from outside who wants to get in, it is worth knowing where to buy and hire camping gear and where you can camp in London.

Not actually in London, but well worth mentioning since they are keen on city members are the **Summit Mountain Adventure Courses,** Little Camberton, Pershire, Worcestershire, Tel: Elmley Castle 240.

Courses including caving, pony trekking, mountain walking, rock climbing, all combined with camping run from July-September. You take your own equipment and pay about £14 a week. This is for people aged 11-15. If you write, you will be sent a brochure.

CAMPING IN LONDON
The **Caravan Harbour** at the Crystal Palace is a very good site. It has hot water and showers, shops and so on. It is always full in the holidays so you should book well in advance if you want to stay there.

CAMPING EQUIPMENT AND CLOTHING
There are a lot of shops where you can buy or hire camping gear. These are some with good stocks:

Hire Service Shops have everything you could possibly need. Their head office is at Essex Road, W3, Tel: 992 0101 and they have a number of branches including 15 Barons Court Road, W14, Tel: 385 1841; 192 Campden Hill Road, W8, Tel: 727 0897; 865 Fulham Road, SW6, Tel: 736 1956; 346 Kings Street, W6, Tel: 748 6740;

Marble Arch Motor Supplies Ltd, 113 Edgware Road, W2, Tel: 723 6695 have a good stock at reasonable prices.

Millets Ltd, 443 Oxford Street, W1, Tel: 629 0666 (other stores in Kilburn High Road, King Street, Portobello Road) are good for cheap surplus clothes.

Youth Hostels Association, 29 John Adam Street, WC2, Tel: 839 1722 are good for advice, equipment, clothes and maps. Some things can be hired, others bought.

CLUB
The **Camping Club of Great Britain** is a really well organised place. They publish a monthly magazine, a list of camping sites and an annual booklet. You can use their sites once you have joined, get advice on camping abroad and take part in their many activities.

EVENT
The **Camping, Outdoor Life and Travel Exhibition** is usually held at Olympia at the end of December

Canoeing

This sport is rapidly becoming one of the most popular in this country. A lot of youth centres organise clubs, so if you don't happen to know of one get in touch with either your local Youth Information Officer or with the **British Canoe Union.**

CLUBS AND CENTRES
The **British Canoe Union** is the governing body of this sport. Although there are rules, they are based on sound common sense and any good

club will be affiliated to the central body. They give advice, run a coaching scheme, organise competitions and run an advisory service.

Islington Boat Club (see under **Boats**)

Leaside Youth Centre is a fabulous club owning about 150 canoes, together with facilities in a well-equipped workshop to build them. The club, open every evening and all day on Saturdays and Sundays, has a good clubhouse for meetings, film shows, lectures, other sports like weight-lifting, and canteen facilities.

Thames Young Mariners has facilities for both canoeing and sailing, but only recognised youth groups can be affiliated to it.

Weekend Canoe Venture organises really good expeditions for people from the age of 12-17. It costs about £4.50 for the weekend.

Welsh Harp Sailing Base is a club open to people of 14-20 who are already members of approved youth organisations. It has a workshop for the repair and maintenance of craft. This centre is open at week-ends, during summer evenings, and throughout the school holidays.

Youth Centres in various parts of London offer tuition in canoeing. It is well worth while enquiring at those near you.

EVENTS

Devizes-Westminster Bridge race at Easter; **National Canoe Exhibition** at the **Crystal Palace** in February.

Careers

Your school is, of course, the best place to get advice from regarding your future. They will be in constant touch with your Youth Employment Officer whose job it is to help you find work and to give you information about the career you hope to follow.

Extremely informative books, published by HMSO, tell you about qualifications, training and opportunities in different fields.

It does happen though, that although you are unable to come up with any good ideas yourself, nothing anyone else suggests really appeals. You can go to the following organisations which give you aptitude tests, intelligence tests and a series of interviews but they each cost around £25:

National Institute of Industrial Psychology, 14 Welbeck Street, W1, Tel: 935 1144

The Tavistock Institute of Human Relations, Tavistock Centre, 120 Belsize Lane, NW3, Tel: 435 7111

If you expect to go to university then the **Advisory Centre for Education** is a good place to know of. They publish material on how to fill in your UCCA form, produce information on different courses at each university.

If you are leaving school and feel that you haven't made much use of your opportunities there, think about evening schools. Buy 'Floodlight'.

You will be staggered at the number and variety of courses run by the ILEA.

Cigarette Cards

At one time only schoolboys seemed to collect these. Now, however, it has become a serious business with a great many people involved in it.

If you already have started a collection or you are genuinely interested, the people to get in touch with are the **Cartophilic Society**.

If you want to acquire tea, trade or cigarette cards, then go to the **London Cigarette Card Company** 30 Wellesely Road, W4, Tel: 994 2346 which has the biggest stock in the world. There is always a chance that you might pick some up in the markets—the Portobello Road, for instance, or Camden Passage—where odd and incomplete sets find their way onto the stalls.

Cinema

Most people know all about Saturday morning cinema clubs but few seem to know that they are organised by the **Children's Film Foundation**. For the ABC Minors Matinees, the Classic Junior Clubs, the Granada Grenadier Clubs and Rank Saturday Clubs the entrance is about 10p. You will probably find details of times and films in your local paper, but if you want general information ring Tel: 930 3374 for Rank cinemas and Tel: 437 9234 for ABC cinemas.

There are plenty of other places showing films:

Commonwealth Institute Cinema, Kensington High Street, W8 shows short films several times daily. These are, naturally, about Commonwealth countries.

Everyman Cinema in Hampstead, like many other cinemas, select particularly good films for children every school holiday.

GLC Parks Department has free open-air cinema shows for you in many of the London parks during the summer. For details buy their pamphlet 'Open Air Entertainment' which is published annually in the spring. It costs 5p, or 7½p by post.

ICA Young Cinema in the Mall shows films on Saturdays and Sundays at 15.00. The price is 25p or 50p for adults.

Imperial War Museum shows films from Monday to Friday at 12.00. On Saturdays the time is 14.45 and on Sundays 16.00. If you are under 12 then you must take an adult with you.

National Film Theatre on the South Bank has programmes on Saturday afternoons and the price for this really super cinema is 30p. In order to go, someone in your family must be a member.

News Theatres are always good for a laugh. They are a good way of filling in time since they show cartoons, short comedies and silent films

40

as well as news reels and so you can go in or out without feeling that to get there at the beginning of a programme is essential.

Eros is at Leicester Square and Shaftesbury Avenue.

Jaceyland is at Baker Street Station and shows Disney films.

Studio Two is in Oxford Street.

Victoria is in Victoria Station.

FILM-MAKING

The following places have facilities for young film-makers.

Cockpit Arts Theatre; Curtain Theatre; Oval House; Theatre Centre. These are all lively places. You will find further details about them in the section on theatre.

Many Youth Centres also offer very cheap facilities for making films. Places like **Cowley Recreational Institute** and the **Earlsfield Youth Centre** really have first class tuition. (You can find further details of courses in 'Floodlight'.)

Clocks

London, like most large cities, has so many clocks in the street that one scarcely notices them. It's true that most of them are just useful but an enormous number of them, both in museums and outside, are so interesting that it's well worth spending a day on a clock-tour.

Big Ben is not in fact the name of the clock. It is the bell that is called Big Ben and it is named after Sir Benjamin Hall who was the Commissioner of Works at the time it was erected. The clock is, of course, famous for its accuracy and the first strokes of the bell actually comes on the hour. Each of the four dials is 24 feet in diameter, the figures are over 2 feet tall, the hands 14 feet and 9 feet long, while the minutes spaces are a foot square.

Curiously enough, there is a replica of Big Ben on the top of a monastery in Peru.

British Museum has the C.I. Ilbert collection. This is considered to be the most important collection in the world. It includes the Strasbourg Tower Clock of 1589, a 14th century iron clock, an Elizabeth carillon, one with moving figures and another that plays tunes on an organ.

Fortnum and Mason always has a small crowd waiting for the hour to strike on the famous clock which took three years to build and necessitated major alterations to the shop itself.

As the clock strikes the 4 foot high figures of Mr. Fortnum and Mr Mason appear from two pavilions. They move forwards, turn inwards and bow to each other. As soon as the clock has stopped chiming a series of 18th century airs such as 'The Lass With the Delicate Air' are played. Mr Fortnum and Mr Mason, once the tunes on the seventeen bells have ended, bow courteously to each other once more and retire to their pavilions where the doors close behind them.

On the second floor of the shop a special viewing window has been built where you can see a great deal of the complex mechanism of the clock.

Greenwich Old Observatory has a number of fascinating old time and astrological instruments on display.

Guildhall Museum houses the superb collection of the Worshipful Company of Clockmakers which demonstrates the history and development of clocks.

Hampton Court has a magnificent clock built to the order of Henry VIII. It not only tells the time but provides a lot of extra information. From it you can tell the date, how many days have passed since the beginning of the year, the time of high water at London Bridge and the phase of the moon.

J. Henry Schröder Wagg merchant bankers, has a fantastic clock in the Banking Hall which is visible from Eastcheap through a large window. It is modern, covers the whole of one wall, and has a small dial in the centre telling the time in London while round the outside it tells the time in every office of the company throughout the world.

King's Cross Station clock came from the Crystal Palace after the Great Exhibition of 1851. It is believed that it is a replica of the one above the Tsar's stables in Moscow.

Liberty's clock in Regent Street has two panels to the right and left, one representing day (a cock) and the other night (an owl holding a rat). In the centre arch of the canopy above the clock is St George and the Dragon. At a quarter past each hour St George chases the Dragon while the bells ring out the Westminster chimes. On the hour he chases the Dragon four times, killing it with his lance at the stroke of the hour bell.

London Museum has an interesting collection of early watches.

National Maritime Museum probably has the best displayed and one of the most absorbing collection of clocks in London.

St Clement Danes' clock plays 'Oranges and Lemons' every three hours.

St Dunstans-in-the-West stands on the site of an early 13th century church. When it was rebuilt and later repaired in 1950, great care was taken to preserve its famous lantern-steeple clock of 1671 with its striking jacks.

St James's Palace clock-tower is one of the surviving parts of the Tudor palace, once the home of the sovereign and destroyed by fire in 1809. It is four storeys high and still has the original doors with linenfold panelling. It is outside this clock-tower that sentries are posted.

Science Museum also has a marvellous collection of early clocks. It includes the Wells Cathedral clock (1392), the Dover Castle clock (14th century), a small replica of the Hampton Court astronomical clock, an Egyptian water clock, and a candle which is striped to mark the hours.

Sir John Soane's Museum contains Sir Christopher Wren's silver calendar watch among a small but surprisingly interesting collection.

Victoria and Albert Museum has a large collection of timepieces showing the history of clocks, including primitive methods of telling the time such as sundials and water clocks. The collection is completely up-to-date since it includes an atom clock. The Chinese and Japanese clocks are particularly interesting.

Wallace Collection contains a really interesting collection, including the 'regulateur' which has intricate astronomical movements, as well as a perpetual calendar.

Clothes

London is littered with boutiques but few of them sell original clothes. What they are offering are clothes which are easily available but in a different environment. We are including those places which have something different to offer as well as places where you might well find good second-hand clothes.

It is always worth keeping an eye open for jumble sales. Sometimes the most amazing things turn up. They do in Oxfam shops where, besides helping yourself, you will be helping someone else.

Antique Bazaar, 6 Church Street, NW8, Tel: 723 7566, has Victorian and Edwardian clothes.

Biba, 124-6 Kensington High Street, W8, Tel: 937 6287, is probably the most famous boutique in London. It is a staggering place where you can buy make-up, shoes, sheets, wallpaper, wrapping paper, posters and a host of other things besides clothes. It will be moving to other premises in Kensington High Street soon so you should check the address.

Bus Stop, 3 Kensington Church Street, W8, Tel: 937 4018 although smaller is still remarkably good value for money.

Chelsea Antique Market, 253 Kings Road, SW3, Tel: 352 1425 has Victorian and Edwardian clothes besides accessories like fans, bags and muffs. Keep an eye open for the Purple Shop since they usually have a good selection, as does Emmerton and Lambert who specialise in old theatrical clothes and uniforms.

Kensington Antique Market, Kensington High Street, W8, Tel: 937 2565 has an astonishing number of stalls selling clothes. These range from things from India, Persia and North Africa to period clothes and mass-produced clothes of today.

Portobello Road always has a lot of old clothes—uniforms, stage clothes, Victorian, cheap Indian and African garments as well as accessories often made by the students who sell them.

Mitsukiku, 73a Lower Sloane Street, SW1, Tel: 730 1505, sells some expensive clothes but has cheap kimonos and other Japanese goods as well.

The Souk, 477 Oxford Street, W1, Tel: 629 6656 is meant to look like a Middle Eastern market. It hasn't come off but it does have a wide range of cheap African and Eastern clothes. It is particularly good for bags, sandals and odds and ends.

Coins and Medals

The coin and medal business is booming. Not only are people interested in them for what they are but since decimalisation they have suddenly realised that they are increasing in value all the time. There are clubs and societies all over the country and they are usually very encouraging towards beginners. The London based ones are the **British Numismatic Society** and **Young Coin Collectors**.

MUSEUMS

British Museum's Department of Coins and Medals, open to students and scholars from 10.00-16.30 on weekdays, has over a million coins alone, while many others are displayed in the Greek and Roman rooms. In the section devoted to Prehistory and Roman Britain is the Snettisham treasure, a hoard of pre-Roman coins. Look too for the Armada medal struck for Elizabeth I.

Imperial War Museum concentrates on the period from 1914 and has a large collection of medals including the relics of members of the armed forces.

National Army Museum has medals up to 1914.

National Maritime Museum has a collection of medals connected with the Royal Navy.

Royal Hospital Museum has a magnificent collection of over 1600 medals, many of them relics of past inhabitants of the Royal Hospital.

Tower of London is the home of the regimental museum of the Royal Fusiliers and contains a good and interesting collection.

Wallace Collection contains a number of bronze medals mainly from the 15th and 16th centuries.

Wellington Museum, housed in the Duke of Wellington's London house, holds many of his relics including a remarkable display of orders and decorations conferred upon him.

MAGAZINES

The following magazines are particularly useful if you are thinking of starting a collection. 'Coin Digest'; 'Coins and Medals'; 'Coins, Medals and Currency Weekly'. By looking at the advertisements you can probably work out for yourself which shops will be of the greatest interest. The markets too are good hunting grounds.

Conducted Tours

It is always interesting to see how things operate. A number of organisations in London offer conducted tours over their premises.

British Rail engine sheds and signal boxes can occasionally be visited at Euston (where you can also see the control rooms), Liverpool Street and Waterloo stations. You must write to the Public Relations Officer of the station you want to visit.

Daily Mail offers tours from Monday-Friday 9.00-23.15. Only people over 14 are accepted. Since they tend to get booked up, write well in advance.

Daily Telegraph organises tours from Monday-Friday 8.30-22.30. These last about 2 hours. Once again, fix it up well in advance.

Electra House is where the world-wide telegraph services are centred. Visits lasting 2 hours are from Monday-Thursday at 10.15, 14.15 and 19.15. Parties are limited to 15 in number. Apply to The Telegraph Manager, Electra House, WC2.

Evening Standard takes parties of 10 around. Minimum age is 15. These tours start at 14.00 and end at 16.00. Fix it up early.

Express Dairy Farm in Regent's Park Road, Finchley has a small museum of ancient delivery vehicles as well as cows and calves. Tours are from Monday-Thursday 2.30—4.30. Apply in writing to Mr. Pierce, Express Dairy, Victoria Road, South Ruislip, Middlesex well in advance.

Faraday Building is the home of the Inland, Continental and International Trunk Telephone Exchanges. Visits lasting 2 hours are arranged for parties of up to 25. From Monday-Friday the tours start at 10.00, 14.00, and 18.00. On Saturdays when the number in the groups is reduced to 15 they are at 18.00 only.

Fleet Building is the home of inland telegraphs. Visits lasting 1 hour take place from Monday-Wednesday at 15.00 (not on Bank Holidays). Parties are limited to 15. Apply to the Chief Superintendent, Fleet Building, Shoe Lane, EC4.

Ford Motor Company at Dagenham organises tours for people over 10 years old. Write to the Public Relations Officer.

Kelvin House is the home of the telephone information service. This is where there are recordings of things like the speaking clock, dial-a-disc and teletourist. Over 15 years for this tour. Apply for visits to the Public Relations Officer.

King Edward Building is concerned mainly with London and Overseas letter mails. You can also see the Post Office Railway here where driverless, electric trains run underground. No visitors are allowed in December but normally parties of up to 20 are taken around on a 2 hour visit on Monday-Thursday from 10.00-19.30 (parties of school children) or from 16.00-19.30 for adults. Write to The Controller, EC/FS (S.B. and A Branch), King Edward Building, EC1.

London Planetarium is hardly in the same category but this is just a reminder that you are, in a sense, conducted through the skies. You can also go into the Battle of Trafalgar where there is a reconstruction of this famous naval battle with a commentary.

Mount Pleasant is the biggest sorting office in the country. Normally open for conducted tours, it is undergoing a major reconstruction which will probably take 2 years to complete.

National Postal Museum is for stamp enthusiasts. A conducted tour lasts about 30 minutes. Normal visiting times are Monday-Friday 10.00-16.30; Saturday 10.00-16.00. Anyone over 11 years is welcome.

News of the World conducts tours on Saturday evenings only. The first is at 19.00 and the last at 22.30. Each tour lasts about an hour.

Roman Fort. Various bits of the Roman Wall can be seen in the city and one of the best parts to see is the west gate. It is open daily 12.30-14.00 on Monday-Friday, but if you prefer to be conducted round in a party get in touch with the Director of the Guildhall Museum.

South-Eastern Sorting Office serves an area of about 50 square miles. Parties of up to 20 are welcome from Monday-Thursday 14.30-19.30 (except in December) and application should be made to the District Postmaster, 23a Borough High Street, SE1.

Stock Exchange is always worth going to. From the heights of the public gallery you can see all the activity going on down below—3000 members all beavering away at once. There is an adjoining cinema where films are shown.

Sun has tours Monday-Friday starting at 8.30 and ending at 22.30. Apply to the 'News of the World' offices for permission.

Telephone Museum in Shoe Lane shows telephones and similar or associated systems from the beginning of this form of communication to today. It contains many working models. It is open Monday-Friday 10.00-16.30. The minimum age limit is 10 years.

Television Gallery is a museum showing a fascinating collection of apparatus which explains the beginning and development of television and demonstrates how programmes are produced and transmitted. This tour takes about 1½ hours and operates Monday-Friday from 10.00. There are four shows a day. This is a place where only those of 16 or over are welcome.

The Times conducts parties Monday-Friday 8.30-22.30. The minimum age is 16. This is yet another place where you need to arrange it well in advance.

War Rooms, several acres of underground passages and rooms, were the centre of operations during the Second World War and the place where Sir Winston Churchill did much of his work. There are two guided tours a day Monday-Friday but it is closed on Bank Holidays.

Western District Office is concerned with the post for the W1 district. The visit which lasts about 90 minutes includes a look at the Post Office railway. It is open from Monday-Thursday 14.30-19.30 (except December) and parties should not exceed 20. Apply in writing to the District Postmaster, Rathbone Place, W1.

Whitefriars Glassworks takes groups of older children around on a glass-blowing tour. Make arrangements well in advance.

Costume

It is astonishing how many early costumes have survived. Every now and again someone goes into an old attic and finds trunks packed with clothes, often in a surprisingly good condition, dating back to the last century or even earlier. Nowadays a lot of people have taken to wearing them and so there are quite a lot on the market. The London museums, however, are packed with a wide-ranging and fascinating collection.

CLUB
Costume Society organises lectures, visits, short courses and even week-end schools.

MUSEUMS
Bethnal Green Museum has a big collection of 18th and 19th century costumes as well as oriental costumes and materials.

British Theatre Museum has a small, interesting collection of theatrical costumes, as well as objects such as Sarah Siddons' make-up table.

Embroiderers' Guild has a collection of historical and contemporary work on display.

Horniman Museum has oriental costumes, primitive tribal masks and gorgeous Temple banners.

Leathercraft Museum is particularly interesting since it concentrates on showing how leather has been used through the ages by the London guilds.

London Museum's collection of royal and ceremonial costumes is fascinating. They also have a good selection of theatrical costumes. In 1972 there is a display of Royal wedding dresses and in 1973 it is planned to have an exhibition on 'London and the Thirties'.

Tower of London has the gold Coronation Robes worn by royalty.

Victoria and Albert Museum is rightly celebrated for its historic costumes. Go straight to the Costume Court where you can see not only the clothes of rich and poor, royalty and tradesmen, but also richly embroidered Church vestments.

SHOPS (see under **Clothes**).

Cricket

PLAYING

National Cricket Association is the body that knows everything. If you simply want to know what's on or if you think you are a fabulous cricketer, get in touch with them. They can fix coaching and also have coaching awards.

Gover Cricket School operates all the year round. Although it is not cheap it is a first class organisation and runs a social club as well.

Central Council of Physical Recreation runs Easter holiday courses. They are divided according to age—either under 13 or under 16.

Crystal Palace, once you become an Authorised User, has nets and you are charged a small amount for the use of equipment.

GLC Parks including Avery Hill, Battersea, Blackheath, Bostall Heath, Dulwich, Eltham South, Finsbury, and Victoria have facilities including nets which you can book for practice. Get in touch with **GLC Parks Department.**

WATCHING

For the best professional cricket go to Lord's or the Oval. For club cricket try Blackheath, Chiswick Park, Kew Green, Holland Park and Wimbledon Common.

MUSEUM

MCC Memorial Gallery at Lord's Cricket Ground is well worth strolling around. It has both interesting and extraordinary exhibits. Apart from being open Monday-Friday it is also open on match days until the close of play.

SCORES

For information on test matches (prospect of play and scores) telephone 160.

EQUIPMENT
Jack Hobbs, 59 Fleet Street, London EC4 Tel: 353 2139
Len Muncer, 139a Park Road, NW8 Tel: 722 9584

Cycling

London is hardly the safest place in the world to go out on a bicycle, so if you have one take advantage of the cycling safety tests organised by the police.

CLUBS
British Cycling Federation is mainly interested in racing. Membership means that you get their handbook telling you of clubs and racing events.
Cyclist Touring Club is a serious body with many groups affiliated to it. They organise rides, longer tours and training courses during the holidays.

EVENTS
Race meetings are held in London at the **Crystal Palace National Sports Centre**, at **Danson Park, Bexleyheath,** at **Herne Hill Stadium,** and at **Paddington Recreation Ground.**

CYCLE HIRE
Hire Service Shops (see **Camping**) for about £1.50 a week.
Savil's Cycle Stores, 97–9 Battersea Rise, SW11 Tel: 228 4279 for approximately £1·25 + 12½p a day. (Both of these shops naturally want a deposit—usually around £5.)

Dance

Most people want to dance but a lot of them feel rather embarrassed about it. We all hate making fools of ourselves in public. Now, however, there are a large number of places where you can learn every possible form of dance.

TAKING PART

Cecil Sharp House offers country dancing, Morris, sword and clog dancing. On Saturday evenings there is a folk dance. It might sound dull but people really have a good time there. There are tea-dances for people of 7-11 on Saturday afternoons.

Cockpit Theatre has a dance-drama group and free improvisation.

Dance Centre is a marvellous place. There are about 135 classes a week for any style of dancing you like to think of. The cost is reasonable, you don't have to sign up for a long course, you can come and go as you wish. They have good teachers, a shop to buy gear at and a magazine 'Move'.

Dance Theatre Commune has special sessions for children. Not particularly cheap but good value for money.

GLC Parks have country dancing, English and Scottish, in Battersea Park, Holland Park, Marble Hill, Parliament Hill and Peckham Rye Park.

London School of Contemporary Dance has classes organised according to age every Saturday morning for people 6-16. 8 lessons each 1½ hours cost £4.20. The lessons are an introduction to the Graham technique.

Oval House has a good dance group for people over 15.

WATCHING

Artists' Place Society which either offers cheap family membership or very cheap youth membership means that you can watch the London Contemporary Dance Workshop rehearsals, meet dancers at social occasions and get priority bookings and special concessions for performances.

Ballet Rambert has special shows in the Collegiate Theatre and sometimes at the Young Vic. Watch particularly for 'Bertram Batell's Sideshow' which is fantastic and has the audience on its feet. Seats are from 40-60p but there is a reduction for parties.

Commonwealth Institute have ballet and national companies performing occasionally. The standard of dance there is very high.

Holland Park for ballet and Spanish dancing held in the open air in June and July usually on Mondays, Thursdays and Saturdays. The London Contemporary Dance Group and students from the Royal Ballet School given performance at Holland Park, usually in July.

Dolls

This section is about old dolls—where to see them and where to buy them. If you are only interested in modern dolls then you won't have any trouble; there are plenty of good toy shops you can go to.

Most small girls treasure their dolls, but some have been kept with such loving care that the doll enthusiast can see them today in museums, almost as they were two hundred or more years ago. Expensive, life-sized dolls, wax dolls, china dolls, rag dolls, cheap wooden dolls—they are all on show. And with them, what is perhaps most fascinating of all, dolls' houses.

MUSEUMS

Bethnal Green Museum has a wonderful collection of dolls and dolls' houses from various countries. The earliest dolls' house was made in 1673, but the dolls are mainly from the 18th and 19th centuries. There is also a selection of rag dolls, and some early cut-out sheets from which they were made.

Gunnersbury Park Museum is a mansion, once the home of the Rothschild family. It contains dolls, dolls' houses and dolls' clothes.

Horniman Museum is the place to go if you want a chance to compare dolls from other countries and races, since the museum is primarily concerned with ethnography. Its collection of dolls is absolutely fascinating.

Kew Palace contains the royal collection of dolls although it is sometimes depleted when some are shown at the Queen's Gallery at Buckingham Palace.

London Museum houses a large collection of dolls from all ages. Among the most interesting exhibits are over a hundred wooden dolls which Queen Victoria dressed when she was a young girl. She gave each one of them a name and these are preserved in the Museum's archives. There are wax dolls which were made to represent her children. Queen Mary's dolls' house, which she played with when she was Princess Mary of Teck, has a dolls' picnic taking place outside the house.

Pollock's Toy Museum has a comprehensive collection which shows the history of doll-making through the ages. On the lower floor the walls are covered with calico printed with 'Little Liz' dolls in mob caps. Among the toys on sale are cakes and trifles for dolls' banquets.

Victoria and Albert Museum contains a collection of dolls of all ages and nations in costume, together with tiny corsets, slippers and mittens. There are also a number of very beautiful 18th century dolls in very good condition. At the museum's bookstall you can buy a booklet on dolls, another about dolls' houses and replicas of early cut-out doll sheets.

Windsor Castle, although not in London, really should be visited by the doll enthusiast. It contains a collection of royal dolls, including many presented to the royal family when on visits abroad. Pride of place goes to the famous dolls' house made for Queen Mary in 1923. The exquisite furniture and accessories, made by superb craftsmen, are all to scale and even include such things as a knife-polishing machine, tiny pots of Shippam's fish paste and a miniature sewing machine that actually sews.

SHOPPING

Antique Hypermarket, 26-40 Kensington High Street, W8, Tel: 937 6911. Kay Desmond at Stand 12 has a good collection of period dolls.

Antique Market, 124 Bond Street, W1, Tel: 629 1819 has an interesting collection of old dolls but they tend to be expensive although in marvellous condition.

Bayly's Galleries, 9 Princess Arcade, Piccadilly, W1, Tel: 734 0180 has a marvellous collection of dolls and things connected with dolls. It is particularly good on period dolls' furniture.

A.S. Clarke Dolls' Hospital, 16 Dawes Road, SW6, is the oldest dolls' hospital in the world. Dolls are mended, restored and nursed back to health, and the hospital also sells dolls at large discounts.

Hummel, 16 Burlington Arcade, W1, Tel: 493 7164 has really beautiful historical dolls but, as you might expect, they are expensive.

Miss Hickman's Doll Shop, 15 Moscow Road, W2, Tel: 727 7880 probably has the finest collection of dolls on sale in London. They range from Victorian and Edwardian dolls to peasant dolls. Not all the dolls are expensive and if you are interested in collecting dolls seriously you will find Miss Hickman very helpful. One of the nice things is that she is always willing, provided there is time, to put on shows for charity.

CLUB

Doll Club of Great Britain is open to anyone who is seriously interested in dolls.

Duke of Edinburgh's Award Scheme

'This scheme is intended to help both the young and those people who take an interest in their welfare. It is designed as an introduction to leisure time activities, a challenge to the individual to personal achievement, and as a guide to those people and organisations who are concerned about the development of our future citizens.'

(H.R.H. The Duke of Edinburgh)

The idea of this scheme is to offer young people a challenge to endeavour and achievement through a balanced programme with a wide choice of leisure activities. Those involved are encouraged to develop existing interests or undertake something new. It is open to 14-21 year olds, and if you want to take part you can do so either on your own, through a youth organisation, or through your school.

There are three awards related to age: Bronze Award for those over 14 years; the Silver Award for those over 15 years; and the Gold Award for those over 16 years. For each award you must qualify in four of five sections: service, expeditions, interests, design for living, physical activity. For example, in the service section for the Bronze Award you might take care of animals, do some community service, learn first aid or life saving. In the interests section for the Gold Award you must follow a leisure interest such as Arts and Craft, Science and Natural History, or outdoor activities, for a total period of eighteen months.

If you are interested, write to the Scheme's head office in London, and they will give you the necessary information.

Famous People

The three best places to go to see how people really looked are very different indeed.

Abbey Museum in Westminster Abbey has a fascinating collection of effigies of people. It used to be the custom for these effigies to be carried in funeral processions and they were made of a variety of materials—wood, leather and wax. Unfortunately many of them have crumbled into dust but those that are left are well worth seeing. There is the wooden one of Edward III who died in 1377, the wax one of Charles II who died in 1685, a copy of an earlier one of Elizabeth I, and many others.

Madame Tussaud's Exhibition, the famous waxworks, has an astonishing collection of the famous and infamous, alive and dead. Infinite trouble is taken to get details right, and so clothes, buttons, spectacles, the way shoes are laced—all are accurate. It is considered a great honour to be included in the exhibition while you are still alive and people are constantly being promoted and demoted as their careers fluctuate and as new arrivals elbow old ones aside. The historical section is fascinating, as much for the accuracy of clothes, materials and accessories as for the physical resemblances.

National Portrait Gallery is a really good place to go. It is the person who was painted rather than the artist that decides who shall be exhibited but many of the portraits are magnificent. By really looking at the faces you can actually trace family likenesses from one generation to the next.

HOUSES AND GRAVES

There are, of course, many people not mentioned in this section. We have chosen on the whole places which are easy to reach or are particularly odd.

Bunhill Burial Fields was probably originally called 'Bonehill' since the bones removed from the Charnel Chapel of Old St Paul's were put here in 1547. It contains the remains of many famous people including John Bunyan and William Blake.

Carlyle's House in Chelsea is the one in which, complaining, he lived for

47 years. It contains many of his relics and has been beautifully preserved.

Dicken's House in Doughty Street is the house in which Charles Dickens lived for a short time. Many of his manuscripts, first editions of his books and other personal relics are exhibited here.

Hogarth's House, is the one in which William Hogarth lived for 15 years. It contains personal relics, impressions of engravings and copies of his paintings. His tomb is in the graveyard of St Nicholas's Church.

Dr Johnson's House is a 17th century house containing relics of the great Samuel Johnson and is, in fact, the place where he compiled his dictionary. His summerhouse, removed from Streatham, is in the gardens of Kenwood House. You can see a statue of him, draped in a Roman toga, in St Paul's Cathedral.

Ben Jonson's tomb is in Westminster Abbey. The story is that he asked for eighteen square inches of ground which Charles I granted him. As a result he had to be buried standing up.

Keats's Museum in Hampstead is the house where John Keats lived. It was either in this garden or on the nearby Heath that he is reputed to have heard the nightingale that inspired his great poem.

Karl Marx has a tomb in Highgate Cemetery. It is vast and incongruous in the setting, but well worth a look. You won't find anything like it anywhere else.

Lord Nelson is buried in the crypt of St Paul's. His coffin was made from the mainmast of a captured French ship, *L'Orient*, and the black marble sarcophagus was originally intended for Cardinal Wolsey. There is an effigy of Nelson in Westminster Abbey Museum but it was not made for a funeral procession. It was made to make money from the curious. On Trafalgar Day there is always a service in his memory at Trafalgar Square.

John Wesley's House and Chapel, an 18th century house opposite Bunhill Burial Fields, contains his furniture, books and other relics. Next to the house is his chapel and behind it the small graveyard where he himself is buried.

Sir Christopher Wren is naturally buried in St Paul's Cathedral. His epitaph, translated, says 'If you would seek his monument, look around you.' As you look, you will realise it couldn't be more apt.

Fencing

If you have ever fancied yourself as a swordsman, you can find out now if you have any ability. The **Amateur Fencing Association** will give you a list of clubs where you can learn and you can also obtain instruction from many of the **Youth Centres** that have sprung up. Places such as the **Battersea Sports Centre**, the **Cowley Recreational Institute** and the **Ensham Youth Centre** offer expert tuition at minimum cost.

Fishing

More people fish than take part in any other outdoor sport and so those of you who are keen anglers probably have your favourite spots, but this list might include some new ones.

PONDS

These places are totally free and there isn't the business of getting a permit: Battersea Park; Clissold Park; Eagle Pond (Clapham Common); Finsbury Park; Hollow Ponds (Whipps Cross); Hampstead Heath Ponds; Tooting Common Lake; Victoria Park Lake; Wandsworth Common.
For cheap fishing try the Crystal Palace Boating Lake (5p).
These places are free provided you get a permit from the Parks Department of the Department of the Environment or the Superintendent of the Park: Bushey Park; Hampton Court Park; Osterley Park; Pen Ponds (Richmond Park); Serpentine (Hyde Park).

RESERVOIRS

Fishing in the Metropolitan Water Boards Reservoirs at Barn Elms, Walthamstow and Walton-on-Thames are only for those of you over 16. Day tickets cost 15p, season tickets £2. You can obtain these either by calling or by post from the Board's Head Office. The coarse fishing season is mid-June-mid-March and you are likely to catch perch, pike and roach. There are special charges at Walthamstow Reservoir for trout fishing from April-September.

RIVER FISHING

Thames fishing is worth while now that fish really are returning to the river. Generally speaking, fishing in the Thames is free from Kew to Staines. Above Staines the price varies from about 10-17½p a day. One very good stretch is between Hampton Court and Kingston Bridge.

CLUBS

You can get information on clubs from the following places: Angler's Co-operative Association; Central Association of London and Provincial Angling Clubs; London Anglers' Association.

SHOPS

There are, of course, shops selling fishing tackle all over London. These are some close to the Thames:
Rangemore Sports, 71 Watling Street, EC4, Tel: 248 5618
Sowerbutts and Son, 151 Commercial Street, E1, Tel: 247 1724
Tachbrook, 224 Vauxhall Bridge Road, SW6, Tel: 834 5179
E. Thurston, 360 Richmond Road, Twickenham, Tel: 892 4175
Tookes Tackle, 614 Fulham Road, SW6, Tel: 736 1484

OBSERVING FISH

If, on the other hand, you are much happier looking at live fish, then these are the places to go:

Chessington Zoo (strictly speaking this is out of London, but you can get there on a Red Rover).

Horniman Museum has an aquarium.

London Dolphinarium where regular performances are given by these intelligent fish.

Regent's Park Zoo where the acquarium is very carefully maintained. Did you know that the water for the sea fish is brought all the way from the Azores, far out in the Atlantic because it is believed that water close to our shores is not pure enough?

Syon Park has a sea-water aquarium filled with fascinating marine life from tropical waters including a young nurse-shark, a porcupine puffer and a clown trigger.

FISHY EVENTS

Fishkeeping and Aquarist Show (Alexandra Palace); Harvest of the Sea Thanksgiving at **St Mary-at-Hill; Swan-Upping on the Thames; Trinity House Service** at **St. Olave's.**

(For further details see **Calendar**.)

Flowers and Plants

Especially during the spring, London's parks and gardens are breathtaking in their beauty. Nothing gives more pleasure than the sight of early crocuses in Hyde Park after a cold miserable London winter. London may be a large city, but it has its own special gardens for botanists, and for all flower lovers.

GARDENS

Apothecaries Garden in Chelsea was planted as a 'physic garden' in 1673. To this day seeds and plants are exchanged throughout the world. You must write first if you want permission to go there.

Avery Hill Winter Garden, built in 1890, is a kind of mini-Kew. There are three plant houses: cool, temperate and tropical. The Cool House has an ornamental pool and fountains in the centre, and a changeable display of decorative plants, including Australian bottle brush plants and camellias. The Temperate House has as a centre-piece a huge palm believed to be over 100 years old, and there is a cactus garden. The Tropical House contains exotic species such as flaming dragon trees, passion flowers and banana trees.

Brockwell Park, a flower garden in Stockwell, once the kitchen garden of a mansion, still has its yew hedges and high walls of red brick. There are pomegranates and magnolia.

Derry & Toms in Kensington High Street has a marvellous roof garden— $1\frac{7}{8}$ acres, 100 feet above the ground. There are even flamingoes stalking about the exotic plants. You can have tea to the accompaniment of six violins, an accordian and a double bass.

Golders Hill Park also contains a garden which was formerly the man-

sion's kitchen garden. It is the finest old English garden in North London.
Ham House, built in the late 17th century, is surrounded by magnificent gardens.

Hampton Court's great attraction is the Maze. You can get in for 1p, or on the inclusive ticket for all parts of Hampton Court for 5p. Although it looks a bit tatty it is surprisingly difficult to get to the centre. To the south of the Palace are the formal Tudor Gardens which reach towards the Thames, and on the East Front in the spring there is a marvellous display of tulips. Don't forget the Great Vine, which still is loaded with magnificent grapes every year, although it was planted in 1769. There are also the King's Privy Gardens, the Great Fountain Court, the Broad Walk and the Wilderness.

Holland Park consists of 55 acres of lawns and gardens and 28 acres of woodland containing exotic and British plants and trees. There is an Irish Garden, a Rose Garden, and a Dutch garden with a wonderful display of tulips.

Kew Gardens is the national botanical garden, containing specimens of over 30,000 plants, 45,000 different types of trees, and over 7,000,000 dried plants and herbs. There is something to interest everyone, from the serious botanist to the flower lover. Every year Kew identifies many thousands of plants, and specimens are exchanged all over the botanical world. As well as its outstanding plant collection and great glasshouses and museums, there are lovely dells and many flowering shrubs. The Queen's Garden, the formal back garden to Kew, was recently laid out in 17th century style, using only plants that were available at that time. In the bowered pergola walk you can see specimens of rare herbs and plants, all carefully labelled with historical quotations.

Peckham Rye Park has American, English and Japanese gardens, and a pleasant stream and water garden.

Queen Mary's Rose Garden, Regent's Park, is named after Queen Mary because of her love of flowers. There are lovely little bowers that line the edges of the garden, and the display of climbing roses makes a wonderful backcloth.

Syon House in Brentford is now the setting for the Gardening Centre. It is a gardener's mecca—55 acres of rose gardens, landscaped gardens, plant display and equipment demonstrations. Towering above it all is Fowler's Great Conservatory, where there is a vast range of exotic and semi-tropical plants, some of which you can buy for your own garden. You can walk through a tropical aviary or trot round the grounds in a horse-drawn charabanc.

Victoria Park is an oasis of beauty in Hackney. The flower garden has a lily pond with a fountain and you approach it through arches of honeysuckle. It is well worth a visit.

MARKETS
Markets which sell flowers are Borough Market, SE1; Columbia Market, Hackney; Covent Garden and Spitalfields (See under **Markets**).

MUSEUMS

Passmore Edwards Museum has a good collection of Essex herbaria, and the Lord Lister herbarium (see also under **'Kew'**).

SHOWS AND EXHIBITIONS

Chelsea Flower show (Royal Hospital Grounds in late May);
Flower Arrangement Association Summer Exhibition (Royal Horticultural Society Hall every other year at the end of June and July);
National Chrysanthemum Society Show (Royal Horticultural Society Hall in early November);
National Rose Society Annual Show (Alexandra Palace in July);
Royal Horticultural Society Hall (exhibitions every Tuesday and Wednesday throughout the year; Great Autumn Show in September).

Flying and Gliding

These, alas, are very expensive sports. A trial lesson at the **London School of Flying** would cost a minimum of £6, while gliding would probably cost a subscription of £10 after the initial entrance fee. If you are really keen, then the thing to do is to join the **Air Cadets**. If you can take the regimentation—although to be fair there isn't so much of it today—then you will probably get the best tuition in the world for free.

Flying Saucers

This is, in fact, an inaccurate heading. The only body in London interested in unidentified flying objects is **BUFORA**, and it really is a serious organisation. They arrange night watches, collect, investigate and compile information and communicate with other similar bodies throughout the world. It's no use thinking that you will try and join just for a giggle—they are only interested in members who want to take a responsible part in the association.

Folk

Folk music is one of the things that seems to have sprung from nowhere and become firmly established very quickly. There are places where you can simply go and listen and others where you can take part.
Cecil Sharp House, the headquarters of the English Folk Dance and Song Society like people to become members, of course, but you can go to the events and classes without being one. Folk singers and musicians are in the Folk Cellar every Saturday night. Every third Saturday it is singers and musicians and dancers together. (See under **Dance**)
Cockpit Theatre have people practising and giving concerts.
Group 64 in Putney has a Sunday night folk club.

Oval House has a folk workshop.
GLC Parks organise events throughout the summer months.

MAGAZINES
The best way of finding out what's on and where is to buy 'Melody Maker' or 'Time Out'.

Food

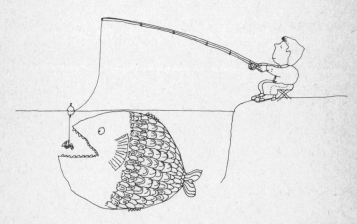

Eating out in London costs a fortune, so if you are planning a day trip it is much better to take your own sandwiches with you, and spend your money on ice cream or soft drinks to finish up. The best ice-creams in London are **Marine Ices**, from 8 Haverstock Hill, NW3 and 370 Cricklewood Lane, NW2. They also have vans which sell ice-cream in parks and tourist spots. Be careful when you buy from other vans in parks and outside public buildings. During the last year prices shot up to an astronomical level.

At certain times of the year and in certain places you can eat free. The **Ideal Home Exhibition** is a good place, though you have to pay to get in first. You can fill yourself three times over with all the samples they provide. Keep an eye open for Food Fairs in big stores where getting in is free at least.

If you must eat out, there are many small cafés in the office parts of London and around the main line stations. Look on the menu in the window for the prices and see if you can afford it before going in. There is nothing more embarrassing than having to walk out once you have sat down. Try and avoid station buffets—their sandwiches are dull and expensive. **Wimpey Bars** are always safe and fairly cheap, but if you are feeling adventurous, find a cheap Italian restaurant and fill up on spaghetti for about 25p. Most big stores have inexpensive buffet lunches. Chain stores are often cheap and reasonably good. Or you can always resort to the old British tradition and buy yourself some fish and chips. The oldest fish-and-chip shop in London is **Malins** of Old Ford Row, Bow.

SOME PLACES TO EAT
Billy's Baked Potato, 88 Chancery Lane, WC2; 18 Coventry Street, W1, is where for about 30p you get a jacket potato with cheese, mince or egg stuffed inside. Very filling and very good.

Ceylon Tea Centre, 22 Regents Street, SW1, is a surprisingly good and calm place to eat. Their salads and cheese flans are 20p up.

Chelsea Drug Store, Kings Road, SW3, is a fairly expensive fun place. All aluminium and glass, it is designed so that you can look down and see what everyone else is doing.

Jolyon branches are all over London. Their sandwiches, snacks or full meals are all reasonably priced—cheap but dull.

Stockpot, 40 Panton Street, SW1; 14 Hogarth Place, SW5; 6 Basil Street, SW3, is a place for good, cheap food, and there is plenty of it. Stockpots are so popular that at lunchtime there are long queues. It is also open in the evenings. For 35-40p you should get two filling courses plus tea or coffee. It is a favourite haunt of students and lower paid office workers.

YWCA, Great Russell Street, WC1, has a cafeteria operating both at lunchtime and in the early evening. Although it is a hostel it is open to the general public as well as the residents. Food is ordinary but good value for money. You can buy hot meals, salads or sandwiches there.

Football

PLAYING
London Football Association will give information about coaching and available pitches.

GLC Parks Department will provide a list of pitches for hire.

Crystal Palace has pitches for Authorised Users at £2 an hour.

WATCHING
All the London professional football clubs have supporters' clubs and some of them have junior sections. It's well worth belonging. It doesn't cost much, travel to away games is cheaper and most of them organise various social activities.

It is sometimes possible to watch teams practising at Arsenal, Chelsea, West Ham and Crystal Palace but you **must** apply in writing well in advance.

CLUBS
London clubs are: Arsenal; Chelsea; Crystal Palace; Fulham; Charlton Athletic; Leyton Orient; Milwall; Queen's Park Rangers; Tottenham Hotspur; West Ham United.

Ghosts, Gibbets, Graveyards
and Gruesome Places

In a city as old as London many ghastly events have taken place. Although it is a long time since anyone was burnt alive, tortured to death or hung, drawn and quartered (and that means exactly what it says; the heads and quarters were later put on public display), the places where these hideous things happened are still there.

Some places like the Tower of London, for example, still have relics but with the march of time—or rather the trample of tourists' feet—they have very little atmosphere left.

We have included some places where ghosts have been frequently reported as having been seen, but if they are there, it is unlikely they will be obliging enough to appear for you. However, ghost hunts are organised by **London Unlimited.**

British Museum is the place to go for mummies of people and animals.

Brompton Cemetery has a number of extraordinary tombs and memorials, many of them astonishingly hideous and amazingly ornate. Look at the inscriptions. Apart from the fact that many of them are amusing, it will give you some idea of how many children died at an early age in the 19th century.

Chislehurst Caves are 12 miles from London and so strictly speaking they shouldn't be included. They have been used since prehistoric times. and you can see the 'deneholes' where people lived. During the Second World War they were used as air-raid shelters.

Cuming Museum, although devoted to the history of Southwark, contains the curious Lovatt collection of London superstitions.

Gibbets where people were publicly hanged were once a place of awe and dread. No one would go past without crossing himself. At times of execution, however, many thousands would fight and push and struggle to get a good look if they couldn't afford a seat in a nearby house or on a specially built stand. These public executions were considered entertainment, and the men who were to die tried to appear brave in front of the crowds.

The most famous of all was Tyburn Tree, now only marked by a small stone at Marble Arch. The other gibbets were on Wimbledon Common, Blackheath and Charlton Park where Hanging Wood was once the haunt of highwaymen.

Hampton Court has its Haunted Gallery. Two ghosts are supposed to walk there. Katharine Howard, executed by Henry VIII, is supposed to rush down the gallery towards the Chapel where she once fled screaming, hoping to see and be forgiven by him. Jane Seymour, who died after giving birth to his only son, is supposed to walk, a lighted taper in her hand.

Hell-fire Caves, at High Wycombe, are some way out of London, but if you want a really weird place, go there. The Hell-fire Club was started by the young and wealthy Francis Dashwood who declared he believed in black magic. In order to make the whole thing more realistic, he hollowed out caves at the foot of a hill. This is a place that really does have atmosphere.

Highgate Cemetery really is a strange place. Dank and overgrown, with coffins visible inside rotting tombs, no wonder people say a vampire haunts it. It has odd memorials and, in the middle of it all, Karl Marx's grave.

Kensington Palace, now the London Museum, is reputed to have the ghost of Princess Sophia, the sad, blind daughter of George III. She liked to spin and sew and it is said that the whirr of the spinning wheel can often be heard.

Madame Tussauds in the Marylebone Road, apart from the famous collection of waxworks, has the Chamber of Horrors with mock-ups of horrible crimes, the guillotine, thumb-screws, the rack and other tortures. It isn't really terrifying with all those helpful, uniformed men around.

St Thomas's Hospital Operating Theatre is in the old chapel of St Thomas's Hospital, now the Chapter House of Southwark Cathedral. It is an early 19th century operating theatre—and you'll get an idea of the crudeness of medicine at that time.

Tower of London, once a place of fear, has a lot of relics. There is Traitor's Gate through which Elizabeth I when still a princess walked, protesting her innocence. Few people who passed through it came out alive. There is the chopping block on Tower Green where the Countess of Salisbury refused to be executed, sparking off a grisly chase, and the execution axe, instruments of torture and Little Ease.

Westminster Abbey is supposed to have a ghost of its own. This is a monk who is seen in the precincts. His feet are just above the level of the paving slabs—an interesting point because they have, of course, been worn away in the passage of time.

Historic London

Perhaps the most important thing to know if you are going to try to see most of the historic buildings in London is that many of them are looked after by the **Department of the Environment (CIO Branch)** and that they issue a season ticket for 37½p. This is a real bargain because it means that there are a number of buildings like Hampton Court, the Tower of London and Westminster Abbey where you can pop in and out as frequently as you like. For adults, of course, the price is double— 75p—but you would probably spend as much as that in one day's viewing.

ORGANISATIONS
Council for British Archeology issues a monthly information sheet saying what excavations are being carried out and what kind of help is needed. At some excavations unskilled people are not wanted, but don't despair. On others they are only too glad to have you. It is important to note that membership is for those over the age of 16.

Southwark and Lambeth Archeological Society is pleased to welcome people under 16 and has a cut-rate membership fee for them. This Society helps at excavations where there is a sudden emergency. There is something to do on most nights of the week at its headquarters at the Cuming Museum.

SOME PLACES TO SEE
Admiralty Arch is a triple-span entrance to the Mall from Trafalgar Square with enormous wrought-iron gates. It was built in 1910 as part of a national memorial to Queen Victoria.

Albert Hall and the **Albert Memorial** opposite are two of the most extraordinarily ugly and ornate monuments to be seen in London. In fact, they are so ugly that people have become quite fond of them.

Aldgate Pump is a drinking fountain (now mains water) built where a pump over St Michael's well used to stand in Leadenhall Street.

Bank of England in Threadneedle Street has a military night guard. It is called the Old Lady of Threadneedle Street and if you look up you will see why. The outside of it is blank and deep down in the vaults are the country's gold reserves.

Banqueting Hall in Whitechapel, designed by Inigo Jones (1622) really was the Banqueting Hall of Whitehall Palace before it was destroyed. It has recently been restored and it has a superb painted ceiling by Rubens. It was from here that Charles I stepped from a window to his execution.

Burlington Arcade, built in 1819, joins Burlington Gardens with Pica-dilly running parallel to Bond Street. It is a tremendously expensive arcade but worth wandering down if only to see the beadles (usually ex-soldiers from the 10th Hussars) whose job it is to see that things are run in an orderly way—no whistling, screaming, racing about and so on.

Canonbury Tower in Islington was once a manor house but all that is left is the tower. It has a marvellous oak staircase that many famous Tudors like Elizabeth I, Sir Walter Raleigh and Sir Francis Bacon have used.

Chelsea Royal Hospital was founded by Charles II and is a lovely build-ing started by Wren with additions by Robert Adam and Sir John Soane. Charles II's statue in the courtyard is by Grinling Gibbons. The pensioners can be seen on parade on Sundays at 10.30 and visitors may go to the 11.00 service in the chapel. The museum, chapel and hall are open to visitors. It is also the setting for the Chelsea Flower Show at the end of May.

Crewe House in Mayfair is a surprise for it looks as if it had strayed there from the country. Everything around it shrieks of the city while this house (1735) with its lawns sits serenly in the middle of the bustle of modern London.

Dean's Yard is on the south-west side of Westminster Abbey and leads to part of the Abbey—the cloisters and the Jerusalem Chamber—but is now used as a playing field by the Choir School of Westminster School.

Downing Street off Whitehall, the street where the Prime Minister and the Chancellor of the Exchequer live, is a quiet, unimpressive road.

Duke of York's column stands on the Mall. He was the Duke who marched his men up and down the hill again. A fantastically extrava-gant man, it was said he was put up on such a high column to escape his creditors. Perhaps it was also to escape the wrath of the army. Every soldier had one day's pay stopped to pay for the monument.

Ely Place, just off Charterhouse Street, has a beadle on duty day and night. It was once the medieval palace of the Bishop of Ely but there is very little left.

Forty Hall is a 17th century mansion now used as a small museum and furnished very carefully. It stands in a superb park with a lake, and there is a courtyard and a stable block.

George Inn, Southwark, the last remaining galleried inn in London, has a double tier of galleries in the courtyard. Once, however, they went right round the whole of the yard because they were the only means of access to bedrooms. It was destroyed by fire and was rebuilt in 1677.

Greenwich Park has the remains of a Roman villa which was discovered in 1902.

Guildhall is the city's civic centre. It has almost been destroyed twice— and, in fact, both times the roof was lost although the walls continued to stand. The first occasion was during the Great Fire of London in 1666, and the second was during the Second World War. It is now used for the election of the Lord Mayor, state banquets and municipal meetings, but at one time it had a very different use. It was the scene of many important trials. Lady Jane Grey who was queen for nine days, Anne Askew who was burned for heresy, and Archbishop Cranmer who was also burned to death were found guilty there and subsequently executed. In the Great Hall the shields of the livery companies are painted round the cornices, while embroidered banners of the 12 great companies hang from the walls. The stained glass windows have scrolls which show the names and dates of the 663 Mayors and Lord Mayors. Gogg and Magog, the legendary giants, 9 feet high carved figures, stand on either side of the Musicians' Gallery. Effigies of them were carried hundreds of years ago in the city's pageants.

Holborn Bars are stone obelisks with silver 'griffins' on the top standing on either side of High Holborn.

Houses of Parliament used to be a royal residence from the 11th-16th century until Henry VIII moved to Whitehall. The Old Palace of Westminster was destroyed by fire in 1834 and this one was opened in 1852. You can always tell when Parliament is sitting because the Union Jack will be flying and there will be a light over Big Ben. You can view the House by writing to your MP or by queuing for admission.

Jewel Tower dates from 1385 and is found just behind Westminster Abbey. It is another part of the old Palace of Westminster and was built to hold the king's private money and jewels. It is surrounded by a moat where goldfish and rainbow trout swim, and inside there is a small collection of things discovered during renovations.

Jewish Museum in Tavistock Square is a well-laid out museum showing public and private worship of the Jews. There are some real treasures to be seen in it including a 13th century Ram's Horns.

Law Courts are really called the Royal Courts of Justice. The Quit Rents Ceremony is held here (see **Calendar**). It is also the turning point of the Lord Mayor's Procession.

Lincoln's Inn was established by the Earl of Lincoln. It has an extremely beautiful chapel with an open undercroft (crypt) where people can wander about. The hall, library and gatehouse (1518) are all worth looking at. The rolls include many famous names such as Sir Thomas More, Sir Robert Walpole and Sir Benjamin Disraeli.

London's Wall survives in part. You can see what is probably the best part in Wakefield Gardens near Tower Hill Underground station. A bit of the wall is actually visible on one of the platforms of the tube station.

Mansion House is the home of the Lord Mayor of London. Built in the first half of the 18th century, it has the Lord Mayor's small court of justice with cells underneath. It is not normally open to the public although there are occasionally special functions when they are admitted.

Marble Arch, standing at the Oxford Street end of Hyde Park, was a mistake. Originally designed by Nash, it was meant to make a splendid entrance to Buckingham Palace, but at the last minute it was discovered that it was just too small for the State Coach to pass through. Now it has tucked inside it a small police office.

Marlborough House was last used by Queen Mary. Since her death, when not being used for official occasions, it is open to the public. It was designed by Sir Christopher Wren for Sarah, the Duchess of Marlborough, but since then it has been enlarged.

Monument (see **Viewpoints**)

Old Bailey is the Central Criminal Court where all the most serious cases are tried. It stands on the site of the old Newgate prison. If you look up to the dome you can see the famous statue with the sword in one hand and the scales of justice in the other. The judges carry bouquets of flowers throughout the summer and sweet herbs are spread around the courts on the opening days of the Assizes. This is a reminder of the old days when the smells coming from the old Newgate prison must have been appalling.

Old Curiosity Shop is in Portsmouth Street behind Kingsway. Although this Tudor house (1567) is always believed to have been the one Dickens wrote about, this has never really been established. The shop is thought to have started life as a dairy for at that time the area was surrounded by meadows.

Old Palace Yard near Westminster Hall has Richard II's statue in it. It was here that Guy Fawkes and the other conspirators were hung, drawn and quartered.

Osterley Park House was built on the site of an Elizabethan building in 1711. Reconstructed by Robert Adam, he designed everything in it—from the ceilings to the carpets. It is set in magnificent grounds with several lakes, stables and outbuildings, which are almost as interesting as the house.

Pitshanger Manor in Ealing, built in 1770, is a house which was bought by Sir John Soane in 1880. In his alterations he included many of the features later found in the house he had built in Lincoln's Inn Fields.

Prince Henry's Room in Fleet Street is believed to have been the Council Chamber of the Duchy of Cornwall under Prince Henry, the son of James I. It dates back to 1610 and its oak panelling and plaster ceilings are typical of the time.

Queen Anne's Gate is a really elegant street of beautiful houses. Look at the fanlights, doorways and window canopies. Outside one of the houses there is a torch extinguisher to be seen. Queen Anne herself stands there.

Queen's House, Greenwich, is in Greenwich Park. It was built for Queen

Anne of Denmark by James I but she died before it was finished. Charles II had it completed for his Queen. It is in Palladian style and is absolutely perfect.

Roman Bath is in the Strand. The origin of it is a mystery. For a long time it was thought to date back to Roman times but now no one is sure. It was restored in the 17th century.

Royal Mint is on Tower Hill. At one time this was the place where the coins of the realm were made—and millions for other countries as well. Now that a new one has been opened in South Wales this one will soon be closed.

Royal Naval College at Greenwich is absolutely breathtaking. When it was finished in 1762 it was a Royal Hospital for seamen but within a very short time it became a training school for Royal Navy officers. The Painted Hall (1703) was designed by Sir Christopher Wren. The Chapel, originally also by him, was destroyed by fire and the present chapel dates from 1779. Much of the wood in the chapel was carved in the naval dockyards at Deptford.

Royal Opera Arcade, one of London's earliest arcades, was built by John Nash in 1816. Although it's tucked away you really should go and look at this marvellous Regency gallery. It has bow-fronted shops, lovely lamps and glass-domed vaults.

St John's Gate is totally unexpected. It is all that is left of the priory of the Order of the Knights Hospitallers of St John. The rooms over the gate are still in use as the headquarters of St John's. It contains a number of interesting relics.

Savoy Chapel is actually the Queen's Chapel of the Savoy. Once it was the chapel in the great Savoy Palace built by the Duke of Lancaster and destroyed in the Peasants' Revolt in 1381. The monarch is actually the Duke of Lancaster and therefore inherited the estate of this once great and powerful family. This is why when the National Anthem is sung the first two lines are:

God save our gracious Queen,

Long live our noble Duke . . . .

It is here that the ceremony of beating the bounds is carried out (see **Calendar**).

Staple Inn is fascinating. Built in 1586, it has Tudor facade and is the only example of domestic Elizabethan architecture. It was once a wool merchants' hostel (which is how it came by the name of 'Staple') and is arranged round two courtyards.

Temple is the name of two Inns of Court. Once it was the property of the Knights Templar but after they were suppressed the legal profession moved in. The Middle Temple Hall where Shakespeare's *Twelfth Night* was first performed was built at about 1570. The serving table is made from the timbers of Drake's ship *The Golden Hind.* The Temple church was originally Norman although it was later added to. The Gatehouse through which you must pass was designed by Sir Christopher Wren.

Temple Bar was built in 1670 to mark the boundary of the City of London. The triple gateway, built in 1672 by Sir Christopher Wren, was moved to Theobald's Park in 1878. The present one, standing at the end of Fleet Street, consists of statues of Queen Victoria and Edward VII with a bronze 'griffin' on the top. It is at Temple Bar that the Lord Mayor customarily meets the sovereign if she is visiting the city. He hands over the sword of state which is immediately returned.

Temple of Mithras was only recently discovered during excavations in Walbrook and was later transferred to Queen Victoria Street. This basilica is nearly 60 feet long. The head of Mithras who was a Persian sun-god can be seen in the Guildhall Museum.

Tower Hill, close to the Tower of London, has a small area of ground with chains round it. This is the place where 75 people regarded as traitors were executed. On the Tower Wharf are guns of all kinds and it is from here that salutes are fired. It is now used as a forum for free speech and it is also here that the Druids celebrate the Spring Equinox.

Tower of London, built by William the Conqueror, was intended to awe the Londoners and indeed, for centuries it was regarded with dread. It has been used as a royal residence, a prison, a mint, a treasury, a menagerie and an observatory.

It is a collection of Norman and medieval buildings, the most massive being the White Tower built by William I from white stone imported from Normandy.

Traitors' Gate was used when prisoners were brought in by water and Queen Elizabeth I herself was forced to use it.

The Bell Tower was used as a prison for many famous people such as the Duke of Monmouth, Sir Thomas More and the old bishop John Fisher.

The Portcullis which is still in working order was meant to be lowered should the rest of the Tower fall and the Inner Ward need to be defended.

The Bloody Tower is best known for being the last known resting place of the two princes in the Tower. Whether the bones found in the 17th century and buried in Westminster Abbey were really theirs is not known for certain. Sir Walter Raleigh was imprisoned here, as was the infamous Judge Jefferys.

Tower Green where the ravens hop about, is the site of many executions. Two of Henry VIII's wives were executed here as were many other famous people.

Beauchamp Tower has many inscriptions scratched on its wall by its famous prisoners. There is a reference there to Lady Jane Grey who saw her husband go to his death and his body being brought back. Later she too went to Tower Green to meet her own death.

Within the Tower there is a marvellous collection of arms and armour as well as the Crown Jewels to be seen.

Trafalgar Square was laid out to commemorate Nelson's victory at Trafalgar and his death, but an enormous number of designs were considered before it was finally started. It was 1852 before Nelson was actually put on the top of his column. There is a story that 14 people dined on the top of the column before his statue was actually erected. **Well Hall** near Eltham Palace was the home of Margaret Roper, the daughter of Sir Thomas More. It is believed that after her father was executed she managed to recover his head from where it was stuck up as warning to everyone else. Only the Tudor Barn is left but it has a magnificent roof and fireplace. Nowadays it is used as an art gallery.

Inter-Action

Dogg's Troupe, Drama-Scapes, Camp-Ins, Act-Ins, Noiseless Movies—these are some of the activities organised by this remarkable trust which believes in participation in the arts and the abolition of barriers between, for instance, actors and audience, the young and the old, teachers and pupils. At the moment it operates from Kentish Town but it has projects going in other parts of London—Paddington, New Cross, Kilburn, Stepney, Wapping and Camden.

Street Theatre takes place in the streets or in large indoor open spaces and people are usually rounded up by Dogg's Troupe. After an exhausting and funny parade usually involving singing and dancing, they reach the play area for game plays which might last from 45-90 minutes.

Prof. R. L. Dogg's Human Flee Circus organises numerous activities—Technicolour Peelers, TV Kits and Clue-Kits among other things.

Act-Ins, also the Prof's work, are improvised events in which the characters might well be members of the audience besides professional members of the troupe. Professor Dogg's activities are, in the main, for people of 9-12, although at times there is a flee circus for everyone as well as one for adults.

Drama-Scapes are another facet of Inter-Action. They are gigantic arts and crafts projects (really gigantic—up to 100 people have worked on some of them). This means that everyone can do something since carpentry, drama, singing, dancing, modelling, painting and song writing are all involved. The Drama-Scapes are centred round a main theme. Once it was Gulliver, another time it was Moby Dick.

Camp-Ins are new. The first one was organised in Camden specifically for people of 12-16. They lived in almost derelict buildings with members of Dogg's Troupe, ran the place themselves, redecorated as much as they wanted to, and acted as play-assistants in some of the other projects.

With any luck you will find them in your area of London and if they do come, join them. Your life won't be quite the same afterwards.

Jazz

PERFORMING

Cockpit Theatre and Arts Workshop has a jazz shop.

Highbury Grove Youth Centre runs evening classes.

London Jazz Association offers all sorts of facilities for young people interested in jazz. Membership is only 15p a year and is open to anyone over the age of 11 who has some instrumental ability. The membership card gets you in at a cheap rate to places like Ronnie Scott's, The 100 Club and The Marquee. Easter holiday jazz courses are organised and there are free classes in various parts of London as well as free rehearsal facilities.

Moberley Youth Centre runs evening classes.

Oval House has a jazz workshop.

Sarah Siddons School runs evening classes.

LISTENING

Battersea Park has performances in June and July, usually on Tuesday at 20.00. It costs about 30p. to get in.

BBC Jazz Club give free tickets to recordings at the Camden Theatre on Mondays.

New Arts Lab has jazz performances.

For further information look at 'Time Out' and 'Melody Maker'.

Jewellery

Most girls enjoy looking at jewellery although very few people can ever hope to own anything really valuable. However, by looking around you can learn enough to make sure that when you do buy something you will end up with something worthwhile. Remember that second-hand jewellery is quite a lot cheaper than new.

BUYING JEWELLERY

There are many antique shops in London but some of the best places with really good selections are the markets. Most dealers are honest. Naturally they want to get as much as they can for their goods but they will not wilfully mislead you. Try to visit the following markets: Antique Bazaar; Antique Supermarket; Bermondsey Market; Bond Street Antique Market; Chelsea Antique Market; Crawford Antique Market; Cutler Street Market; Hampstead Antique Emporium; Kensington Antique Market; Portobello Road Market.

LOOKING AT JEWELLERY

These are the best places to see jewels:

Abbey Museum in Westminster Abbey has replicas of the Crown Jewels as well as other exhibits including the cameo ring Elizabeth I gave to the Earl of Essex.

British Museum contains Egyptian, Greek and Roman jewellery, the beautiful finds from the Sutton-Hoo burial ship, medieval and 17th century exhibits.

Geological Museum has a fine collection of gem stones. When you have looked at them in their natural state you will realise how much depends on those who cut the stones, the designers and the craftsmen who actually make jewellery.

Goldsmith's Hall has a really fabulous collection of antique plate, modern silver and jewellery.

London Silver Vaults has the largest collection of silver in the world as well as some superb jewellery.

Natural History Museum has minerals and stones.

Tower of London has in its newly constructed stronghold the Crown jewels. There are so many and some are so massive that it's hard to believe that they are all real.

MAKING JEWELLERY

If you become seriously interested in making jewellery there are a surprisingly large number of classes available. Get in touch with your local **Youth Centre** or buy 'Floodlight'.

The Gemmological Association supplies crystal specimens and ornamental materials. (See under **Art and Craft** for shops that sell materials for making jewellery.)

Judo

Judo is flourishing in London. There are a great number of clubs and evening classes where you can learn. The governing body, the **British Judo Association** will answer any enquiries and can put you in touch with your nearest club. British Junior trials are staged at the **Crystal Palace** in February.

The Budokwai at GK House, Gilston Road, SW10 has a junior judo section for people who are over 8 years old. A three month's course costs £4.50.

Markets

One of the best things about London is its markets. They are, generally speaking, lively, noisy, good-humoured and amusing. They divide into two main kinds; wholesale, which sell to the trade, and retail which sell directly to the customers.

WHOLESALE MARKETS

To see these at their best you need to get up really early. By lunch-time there is almost nothing to see. Most of the trading goes on in the early hours of the morning.

Billingsgate is London's famous fish market. Although the charters and acts relating to it go back to 1400, there was certainly a market there long before that. Watch for the porters with their traditional flat leather and wooden caps. It is open from 6.00.

Covent Garden is the biggest fruit, flower and vegetable market in London. Once it was part of the convent of Westminster and it is thought that many of the monks are buried there. Right in the middle is St Paul's Church (known as the actors' church) with its small green churchyard. The market is alive at night and by 9.00 almost all activity is coming to an end. A new market is being built at Nine Elms and it seems that this historic market will close in the near future. It is open all night.

Leadenhall Market really shouldn't be included in this section at all. It was originally the wholesale poultry market but now it has become a retail one with over seventy shops. It is a great late Victorian iron and glass building.

Smithfield deals in meat, poultry and provisions and is the biggest meat market in the world, covering 10 acres and with 2 miles of shop frontage. Originally it was called 'Smooth Field' and it has been used for tournaments, executions and fairs. Watch for the statue of Henry VIII. It is the only one in London.

Spitalfields is the Corporation of London's fruit and vegetable market with the Flower Market and the Fruit Exchange next to it. The main market frontage is over 1½ miles long. It was established in 1682 although there was trading there much earlier when it was centre of the silk industry. It starts work in the early hours of the morning.

RETAIL MARKETS-OUTDOOR

Bermondsey Market, formerly the Caledonian Market, operates only on Fridays 6.00-13.00 but by 10.30 there isn't a great deal left. Dealers do a lot of their buying there and you will find all sorts of things including silver, jewellery, watches, furniture and bric-à-brac.

Berwick Street Market is in the middle of Soho. It is open every day and sells fruit, vegetable, fish and poultry all mixed up with household goods.

Borough Market, under the arches of London Bridge Railway, is a good, cheap fruit and vegetable market which opens at 6.00 every weekday.

Camden Passage in Islington is an open antique market with shops on either side of the passage where dealers know what they are selling. It is not particularly large but it is in an interesting part of London, especially with the canal nearby. This is a Saturday market only.

Chapel Market open on weekdays except Thursday, and on Sunday mornings, is a mixed market—fruit, flowers, vegetables, old clothes, junk and household goods.

Club Row near Petticoat Lane is open only on Saturday mornings from 8.00—13.00. Carefully inspected by the RSPCA, it sells animals, birds, fish and occasionally reptiles at one end of it. The other end has china, haberdashery and general household goods.

Columbia Market in Hackney is open only on Sunday mornings for the sale of flowers and plants.

The Cut near Waterloo Station is a general market selling basically fruit, vegetables and household goods but there are some odd stalls with bits of radio equipment, plants, books and so on. It is open every day from Monday to Saturday.

Cutler Street is a specialist market for silver, coins and jewellery. A lot of dealers use it and it usually has very interesting items.

East Street in Walworth, closed on Mondays and Thursday afternoons, is a household-type market but at the far end of it there is quite a lot of junk which is worth picking over. Try going there on Sundays. It is particularly good for flowers and fruit then.

Farringdon Road, although open on weekdays, is at its busiest on Saturdays. It specialises in books and prints.

Inverness Street in Camden Town is small, and really only sells food and household goods, although on Saturdays there is the odd junk stall around.

Leather Lane in Holborn is a small general market open only from Monday to Friday from about 10.30 to 15.00.

Petticoat Lane rightly has a marvellous reputation. The patter of stall-holders really shouldn't be missed. Open only on Sunday mornings it is always crowded and noisy. It sells household goods mainly but you'll find clothes, modern junk, jewellery, records and food as well.

Portobello Road is open every day of the week except on Sundays and Thursday afternoons as a fruit and vegetable market, although it really comes into its own as an antique and junk market on Saturdays. There are do-it-yourself people selling candles, jewellery and leather goods as well as young and old singing and playing instruments. Always crowded and noisy, it is well worth a visit.

Totters Market in Middlesex Street is the place the rag and bone men come to sell the junk they've picked up in the week. It is open on

Sundays 7.00-16.00. If there are any bargains, they are snatched up early.

Uxbridge Road in Shepherd's Bush is open daily. Busiest on Saturdays, it is a large general market.

Vallance Road near the Whitechapel Road is a good junk market but you need to get up early if you hope to find a bargain. It operates from 5.00.

Walthamstow High Street is open every weekday except for Thursday afternoons. Although on the whole it sells all sorts of food it is packed with stalls selling anything from books to electric light bulbs.

INDOOR MARKETS

Most of the indoor markets are antique markets—but this doesn't mean everything is expensive. Each one has a lot of different stalls inside, most of them specialising in something, and they are well worth looking round.

Antique Bazaar is quite small and tends to have quite nice things like fans, brooches and handbags. It has books and prints besides some Victorian clothes.

Antique Supermarket is just off Oxford Street. It is very large with dozens of stalls and has almost everything—furniture, rings, pictures, prints, clothes and so on.

Bond Street Antique Market is good for jewellery, toys, dolls and small ornaments—but it tends to be expensive.

Chelsea Antique Market is huge and has got everything. There are some good clothes stalls as well as theatrical and oriental ones. It's a noisy, but busy place that's fun to go to.

Crawford Antique Market, not far from Baker Street, is good for collectors of furnishing antiques. It has very little in the way of cheap odds and ends.

Hampstead Antique Emporium, a very attractive place, is in a yard near the tube station. It mainly sells antiques for the house and garden although there is some jewellery as well as odd curios.

Kensington Antique Market has antiques and jewellery as well as bags, belts, records and posters. It is particularly good on clothes—Indian, second-hand, home-made, Victorian and Edwardian—they are all there.

Matchbox Labels

A lot of people now take matchbox label collecting very seriously. If you are really interested and have started a collection or are thinking of starting one get in touch with the **Matchbox Label Society**, which organises lectures and produces a quarterly magazine.

Models

A great number of people take model-making very seriously and there are a great number of shops in London devoted to the business. For looking at models the best places to go are:

MUSEUMS
Bethnal Green Museum which has, amongst other exhibits, a scale model of the Duke of Windsor's saloon car used on his tour of India.
Imperial War Museum has a collection of models connected with the military. It is particularly good on ships and aircraft.
National Maritime Museum has a really comprehensive collection of ship models.
Science Museum is crammed with models, many of them working.
Trinity House has a number of ship models. Admittance is by application to the Warden.

SHOPS
Aeronautical Models, 39 Parkway, NW1, Tel: 485 1818
Beatties, 10 The Broadway, W14, Tel: 886 4258, 112 High Holborn, WC1, Tel: 405 6285 (for model railways and cars)
Bonds, 186 Tottenham Court Road, WC1, Tel: 636 3025 (for transport models)
Bond's O'Euston, 357 Euston Road, NW1, Tel: 387 5441 (for model engineering tools)
Cherry's, 62 Sheen Road, Richmond, Tel: 940 2454 (for steam engines)
Hamleys, 200 Regent Street, W1, Tel: 734 3161 (particularly good for model railways)
Hummel, 16 Burlington Arcade, W1, Tel: 493 7164 (for toy soldiers and military models)
Langford Galleries, 11 Charterhouse Street, EC1, Tel: 405 6401 (for model pre-1930 ships)
Model Railway Manufacturers, 14 York Way, N1, Tel 837 5551
Henry J. Nicholls, 308 Holloway Road, N7, Tel: 607 4272 (for radio controlled aircraft)
Ripmax, 39 Parkway, NW1, Tel: 485 1818 (for boats and trains)
W & H (Models), 14 New Cavendish Street, W1, Tel: 935 8835 (for model railway equipment)

MAGAZINES:
'Aeromodeller'; 'Model Boats'; 'Model Cars'; 'Model Engineer'; 'Model Railway Constructor'; 'Model Railway News'

Motor Cycles

The **Auto-Cycle Union** is the governing body of this sport and its Handbook lists all motor-cycle clubs and events. Together with the RAC it organises proficiency training schemes. If you hope to own a motorbike at some point you would be well advised to get in touch with this organisation.

EVENTS

Speedway is staged at the **Crystal Palace, Hackney Stadium, West Ham Stadium** and **Wimbledon Stadium**; The veteran motor-cycle and tricycle run to Brighton is an out-of-town event but enthusiasts shouldn't miss it. It starts at Tattenham Corner Station at about 8.30 and is usually held in March.

For out-of-town speedway, go to **Brands Hatch.**

Music

There is so much going on in the music world in London that it is difficult to know where to begin. No matter how badly off you are, if you want to play an instrument there will be a class available for you to go to. If you want to sing in a choir, there are plenty of these, but the standard is very high and you will be expected to take it seriously. If you simply want to listen there's plenty of opportunity for that too. **Folk** and **Jazz** are in sections of their own.

LISTENING

For free concerts at lunch-time, go to the following churches:

Holy Sepulchre, Holborn Viaduct: Wednesday 13.15.

St Botolph Without, Bishopsgate: Thursday 13.10

St Bride's, Fleet Street: 3rd Thursday in month 13.15.

St Lawrence Jewry, Gresham Street: Wednesday 13.00 (not in August)

St Martin-in-the-Fields, Trafalgar Square: Thursday 13.05

St Mary-le-Bow, Cheapside: Monday-Friday 13.05 (for recorded music); Wednesday 13.15 (for recitals)

St Mary Woolnoth, Lombard Street: Friday 13.05 (Singers' workshop rehearsals)

St Michael-upon-Cornhill, Cornhill: Monday 13.00

St Olave's, Hart Street: Friday 13.05

St Stephen's, Walbrook: Friday 12.30

Do check times because these might well vary.

For cheap indoor concerts:

Ernest Read Concerts, held in the Royal Festival Hall for children, have become an institution. These are given from October to May on Saturdays approximately once a month. There is always a special Christmas concert and there are other holiday concerts given in the Purcell Room.

Robert Mayer Concerts are equally famous. Intended for people round about the age 10-12, they too are given in the Royal Festival Hall. Usually about six are given between October and March with a special one with carols in December.

Commonwealth Institute has performances and these are sometimes free.

CLUBS AND CENTRES

Finchley Children's Music Group is an organisation with a very high standard concentrating on choral singing. The Junior Choir is for under 12s, Senior Choir for 12-18s. Membership costs £1 a year and the Group meets on Sunday afternoons. The choirs frequently have professional engagements.

Horniman Museum not only has a collection of musical instruments from all over the world but it arranges free lectures on Saturday afternoons at 15.00.

London Orchestral Association will put you in touch with teachers if you want to take up an instrument.

London Symphony Orchestra Club has a moderate subscription and this enables you not only to attend lectures usually given in Holborn Central Library, but to attend final rehearsals and to obtain greatly reduced tickets for performances.

Young Music Makers which operates from Golders Green gives singing and instrumental lessons to 3-14 year-olds on Saturday mornings at Primrose Hill School and on Saturday afternoons at Gospel Oak School. Cost of individual tuition varies from £2.50 for 12 weeks in Junior Singing to £5.25 for 12 weeks of Guitar tuition. Pupils are encouraged to join orchestras and bands.

Youth and Music is an organisation for people aged 14-25 which gives you the chance to go to ballet, opera and concerts at greatly reduced prices. This is for group membership only.

MUSICAL INSTRUMENTS TO SEE

British Piano and Musical Museum has a quite remarkable collection of instruments. You should be accompanied by an adult if you want to visit it.

Fenton House Museum, a beautiful Hampstead house built in 1693, contains a collection of early keyboard instruments.

Horniman Museum—see above

Royal College of Music has over 400 string, woodwind and keyboard instruments, mainly European in origin but some from the Near and Far East.

Victoria and Albert Museum has a good collection of keyboard instruments.

MUSICAL EVENTS

St Paul's Cathedral has the *St Matthew Passion* on the Tuesday in Holy Week after Advent Sunday and the *Messiah* in November.

Henry Wood Promenade Concerts at the Royal Albert Hall (although occasionally given in places like the Royal Opera House and the Roundhouse) start at the end of July and go into September. First and last nights are almost carnival nights.

Open-air concerts in the summer at Crystal Palace, Kenwood and Holland Park. (For further information apply to **GLC Parks Department**.)

ELECTRONIC MUSIC groups for beginners and others are held at the **Cockpit Theatre**.

COUNTRY AND WESTERN performances are given in the Spring and Late Summer Bank Holidays in **Battersea Park** at 15.00 and 19.30 besides a festival at the **Empire Pool and Stadium, Wembley** at Easter, (For other performances get in touch with **GLC Parks Department**.)

POP
The **Crystal Palace Concert Bowl** was the venue for fantastic concerts in 1972 and plans for bigger and better ones in 1973 are well under way. For these and other occasions look in the musical press.

Natural History

Those interested in natural history should also see under **Animals and Birds** and **Flowers and Plants**. This section deals with natural science generally, and includes anything that doesn't fall into those two categories.

London Natural History Society welcomes Junior Members at all indoor and outdoor meetings, and Senior Members are always willing to give you help and advice. There are special sections for Botany, Ecology, Entomology, Geology and Archeology, Ornithology, Ramblers and an Epping Forest Field Section. Indoor meetings are held at Holborn Central Library, Theobalds Road, or at the Co-operative Hall, Bath Road, Hounslow if you join the S.W. Middlesex Section. At formal indoor meetings members take along natural history specimens and photographs and report observations. There are illustrated talks and films. At informal meetings members exchange ideas and talk generally. There are field meetings every weekend where you do things like bird surveys, surveys of vegetation, water, soil, rabbit population, plants, etc, or practical work on pottery, identifying and analysing bones and shells, archaeology. Junior Members (under 18) pay a yearly subscription fee of £1.25. There are reductions for family members. Two publications, the 'London Naturalist' and 'London Bird Report' are sent to all members, and you can join the Reading Circle to obtain copies of specialised magazines by circulation. For full details of membership write to A. J. Barrett, 40 Frinton Road, Kirby Cross, Frinton-on-Sea, Essex.

MUSEUMS
Broomfield Museum is an ancient mansion in Palmer's Green with a natural history collection.
Butler Museum is an interesting place with a natural history section which includes a herbarium, British and tropical butterflies and British birds.
Epping Forest Museum contains a natural history collection relating to the animals, birds and plants in Epping Forest and man's connection with them. The object of the Museum is conservation.
Geological Museum is concerned with the principles of physical geology, regional geology of Great Britain, and the geology and mineralogy of the world. There is also a relief globe of world geology, and a fascinating model of Vesuvius erupting at regular intervals.
Greenwich Borough Museum's natural history collection is specifically related to the district.
Horniman Museum deals with the study of man and the effect of his environment. There is a natural history section that is well worth a visit. Among the exhibits are an aquarium and a beehive.
Kew Gardens is famous for the natural collections, identifications of rare plants and research. (See under **Flowers and Plants** and **Parks**.)
Natural History Museum is the home of the national collection of animals, plants, birds, fish and insects, also has exhibits of rocks and fossils, evolution etc. For details of the Children's Centre, see under **Animals and Birds**.
Passmore Edwards Museum contains a large collection dealing with the natural history of the district.

SHOPS
Aquaria, goldfish, tropical fish, plants and everything else for the aquarist can be bought at:
Fish Tanks, 49 Blandford Street, W1, Tel:935 9432
Tachbrook Tropicals, 244 Vauxhall Bridge Road, SW1, Tel: 834 5179
Queensborough Fisheries, 111 Goldhawk Road, Shepherds Bush, W12, Tel: 743 2730
Bees and beekeepers' supplies can be bought at:

Robert Lee, Beehive Works, George Street, Uxbridge, Tel: 89-33181
Butterflies can be bought at:
London Butterfly Centre, 523 Oxford Street, W1, Tel: 629 0419
Fossils, rocks and shells can be bought at:
Gregory Bottley, 30 Old Church Street, SW3, Tel: 352 5841;
Eaton's Shell and Rock Shop, 16 Manette Street, W1, Tel: 437 9391
Minerals can be bought at:
Gregory Bottley, 30 Old Church Street, SW3, Tel: 352 5841;
Max Davis, 38 Oxford Street, W1, Tel: 580 7571;
Gemrocks, 7 Holborn, EC1, Tel: 405 6786.

MAGAZINES
'The Aquarist and Pondkeeper'; 'Entomologist's Monthly Magazine';
'Geological Magazine'

Needlework

If you are keen on sewing you probably learn it at school, but enthusiastic girls—and boys, perhaps—can do a postal dressmaking course run
by the **Institute of Domestic Arts.** This costs at least £7.35, so if you
want something cheaper, look in 'Floodlight' for evening classes. (See
under many local **Youth Centres.**)

MUSEUMS
Bethnal Green Museum contains a wonderful collection of Spitalfields
silks, designs and fabrics.
The Embroiderers' Guild has an interesting exhibition of old and contemporary embroidery.
Ham House has a collection of embroidery, including a rare 17th century altar cloth, and other exhibits including tapestries and carpets.
Horniman Museum displays a collection of primitive textiles.
Royal School of Needlework has a large collection which is worth
visiting.
Victoria and Albert Museum has fine collections of embroidery, woven
fabrics from Egyptian to modern times, and textiles from the Far East
and Europe. The most important tapestries in London are also housed
here, marvellous samples of embroidery, including Charles I's military
scarf, and a collection of carpets.
William Morris Gallery contains Morris designs of woven wool fabrics
and chintzes.

SHOPS
Most of the big stores have good fabric and trimming departments for
the needlewoman. Some of the best are:
John Lewis Oxford Street, W1, Tel: 629 7711, has a wide range of
materials at reasonable prices.
Dickins & Jones, 224 Regent Street, W1, Tel: 734 7070.

Harvey Nichols, Knightsbridge, SW1, Tel: 235 5000
Listed below are some of the more unusual places:
R. D. Franks, Market Place, Oxford Circus, W1, Tel: 636 1244
Specialists in sewing-room equipment—tracing wheels, all kinds of scissors, tailor's chalk and other aids.
Liberty's, 210-220 Regent Street, W1, Tel: 734 1234 is famous for fabulous silks and individual designs in prints. Occasionally bags of pieces are sold—fabulous for patchwork.
Needlewoman Shop, 146 Regent Street, W1, Tel: 734 1727 sells everything for the needlewoman. You can get advice on a variety of things such as tapestry, embroidery and patchwork.

SEWING MACHINE HIRE
If you haven't got a sewing machine, you can hire one by the week from **Sew Fashions Ltd,** 130 Ewell Road, Surbiton, Tel: 399 0111; **Sewing Machines Sale and Hire,** 513 Hackney Road, E2, Tel: 739 7954. Some branches of **Singer's** hire machines but you need to book one in advance.

Odds and Ends

London is so packed with things to see and do that the real problem is finding enough time to fit everything in—and some things, like these below, really don't seem to fit into any specific category yet they shouldn't be missed.
Beaver House was the headquarters of the Hudson Bay Company and here is a fascinating collection of handicrafts and relics of the North American Indians.
Bow Bells, in the church of St Mary-le-Bow, destroyed once in the Great Fire of 1666 and again in 1941, were recast using fragments of the old ones and hung in 1961. Unless you are born within the sound of them, you cannot be considered a Cockney.
Cleopatra's Needle, on the Embankment, not far from Charing Cross, is nothing whatever to do with Cleopatra. It was erected in 1878 after a hazardous journey from Egypt and the Victorians put a number of curious things beneath it including a portrait of Queen Victoria, a verse from St. John's Gospel in 215 languages, English coins and a rupee, a translation of Genesis into Arabic and a newspaper of the day.
Clink Street which runs down to Bankside has given us the word 'clink'. The Liberty of the Clink was a manor outside the jurisdiction of the City. Later it was the site of the prison for Southwark.
Crosby Hall is a building which incorporates the great hall of Crosby Place and was occupied by Richard III at one time. It was brought from Bishopsgate where it used to stand and was erected on this site in 1910. The effigies of Sir John Crosby, who built it, and his wife can be seen in St Helen's Church in Bishopsgate.
Dick Whittington's Stone in Highgate is the place where he was

supposed to have sat and heard Bow Bells telling him to 'turn again'. A nearby pub has a plaster cat on top of it. Look at the stained glass windows in Westminster Abbey. In one of them you will see him and his marmalade cat.

Fat Boy in Cock Lane is a gilded cherub set high on the wall of this street. It marks the most northerly spot reached by the Great Fire of London of 1666.

Frances Stuart's parrot, stuffed, of course, can be seen together with her effigy in the Abbey Museum. She can be seen as Britannia on old pennies.

The Guildhall Museum is the place to be at 9.00, 12.00, 15.00 or 18.00 for, on the hour, a carillon plays English, Irish, Scottish, Welsh, Australian and Canadian tunes.

Henry VIII's Wine Cellar was actually built for Cardinal Wolsey. It can only be visited by receipt of a pass from the Secretary of the Department of the Environment.

Holy Sepulchre has a bell which was rung outside the cell of a condemned man in Newgate prison.

Insurance Museum has insurance companies' firemarks, helmets and fire-fighting equipment on view.

Lancaster House contains a 3rd century Roman boat found on the site of County Hall. You can only see it on application to the Director of the Museum.

23 & 24 Leinster Gardens, Bayswater, aren't really houses at all. The fronts are dummies built to preserve the appearance of the road when the Circle line was being constructed.

London Stone in Cannon Street is set into the wall of the Bank of China. It is believed that it was from this stone that the Romans measured all the distances in the British Isles.

Liverpool Street Station is built over an old plague pit.

King Lud and his sons are 16th century figures who used to stand at Ludgate until it was demolished. They were transferred to the church of St Dunstan's-in-the-West which also has a contemporary statue of Elizabeth I over the vestry porch.

Mayfair got its name because from about 1688 a fair was held in May in Shepherd's Market.

Postman's Park is the churchyard of St Botolph's in Bishopsgate. Tile tablets recall accounts of bravery during the 19th century.

A Roman pavement can be seen in Ironmonger Lane. It is in the premises of Messrs. Peat, Marwick, Mitchell & Co. who will almost certainly show it to you if you write to them.

St Botolph's Aldgate has, although it is not generally on view, the mummified head of the Duke of Suffolk, the father of Lady Jane Grey.

St James Garlickhythe has iron hat racks and sword rests.

Sir John Soane constructed the cell of an imaginary monk, Padre Giovanni. Close by are the catacombs and the Sepulchral Chamber with Seti I's alabaster sarcophagus. It is all in his museum.

Sloane Square underground platforms are under the Westbourne river. This river flows into the Serpentine and from there it is carried into the Thames.

South Kensington has the fossilised trunk of a giant conifer which stood outside Edinburgh and is 27,000,000 years old. (You will find it by going through the subway leading from South Kensington tube to the museums and then taking the first exit on your left.)

At Vintner's Hall five cheers are given instead of the customary three. This is commemorate of the day when five kings (Denmark, England, France, Cyprus, Scotland) all dined together in 1363.

Waterloo Place, at the far end of Regent Street, has a number of stone blocks on the pavement. They were used as mounting blocks.

Whitefriars Crypt is beneath the 'News of the World' offices. It was the crypt of a Carmelite House and has been beautifully restored. Apply to the newspaper for permission to visit it.

One O'Clock Clubs

One o'clock clubs are for children under five. They are run by experienced play leaders and are open 13.00-17.30 each weekday throughout the year. Mothers must accompany their children to the club, but they are free to join in or rest, as they choose. Any child under five can join in, and everything is free. Activities include water and sand play, modelling, doll and puppet making, painting and drawing. On fine days children play in the open air; on wet days there is a special hut available. Every one o'clock club is affiliated to the Royal Society for the Prevention of Accidents and is a Tufty Club—with the object of encouraging road safety. Listed below are current one o'clock clubs. However, these are bound to change from time to time, and new ones will be added. For up-to-date information you can get in touch with the **GLC Parks Department**.

Barnsbury Park, Barnsbury Road, Islington, N1
Battersea Park, Albert Bridge Road, SW11
Beckenham Place Park, Old Bromley Road, SE6
Brickfield Gardens, Clemence Street, E14
Brockwell Park, Arlingford Road, Tulse Hill, SW2
Charlton Park, Charlton Park Road, SE7
Clissold Park, Green Lanes, N4
Crystal Palace Park, Crystal Palace Park Road, SE19
Geraldine Mary Harmsworth Park, St George's Road, SE1
Haggerston Park, Edith Street, Shoreditch, E2
Holland Park, Holland House, Kensington, W8
Kennington Park, St Agnes Place, SE11
Kensington Memorial Park, St Mark's Road, W10
Leyton Square, Peckham Park Road, SE15
Little Wormwood Scrubs, Scrubs Lane, NW10
Margaret McMillan Park, Watson's Street, New Cross, SE8
Millwall Park, East Ferry Road, Cubitt Town, E14
North Camberwell Open Space, Addington Square, SE5
Parliament Hill, Highgate Road, Kentish Town, NW5
Peckham Rye Park, Junction of Peckham Rye and Homestall Road, SE22
Ravenscourt Park, King Street, Hammersmith, W6
Slade Gardens, Robsart Street, North Brixton, SW9
Southwark Park, Southwark Park Road, Rotherhythe, SE16
Springfield Park, Springfield off Upper Clapton Road, E5
Telegraph Hill, Pepys Road, New Cross, SE14
Wandsworth Common, Dorlcote Road, SW18
Wapping Gardens, Greenbank, Wapping, E1

Palaces

Everyone always thinks of a palace as something turreted, perhaps surrounded by a moat, and built high on a prominence. London's palaces simply aren't like that at all. They tend to look like large houses, now rather sadly dwarfed by the high buildings around them. Not only royalty lived in palaces. It is also the name given to the place where high dignitaries of the church live.

Buckingham Palace is now the permanent home of the sovereign. You can always tell whether the Queen is there because if she is, the Royal Standard is flying. At one time the royal palace was in Whitehall, but after it was burned down St James's Palace was used. It was Queen Victoria, whose statue faces Buckingham Palace, who picked on that house as the royal residence. It was originally built in 1703 and in 1825 it was remodelled by Nash. Its grey stone facade was added in 1825. The only parts of it open to the public are the Royal Mews and the Queen's Gallery.

Eltham Palace was actually used as a royal palace up to the time of Henry VIII. There is a 14th century bridge over the moat.

Fulham Palace is the residence of the Bishop of London and is a magnificent building standing in its own park on the banks of the Thames. It is possible to visit it at certain times.

Hampton Court really shouldn't be included since it is some way out of London, but it is possible to get there on a Red Rover. Built by Cardinal Wolsey and presented by him to Henry VIII in an effort to regain the king's favour, it is a marvellous example of a Tudor building. There's a lot to look at but don't miss the Maze, the formal flower gardens and the Great Vine.

Kensington Palace in Kensington Gardens is now the home of the London Museum. It was first used by William III in 1689 but parts of it are a lot older.

Kew Palace sounds rather grand but actually it is a small brick house inside Kew Gardens. It was built in 1831 and contains relics of George III, and, curiously enough, a collection of animal and bird pictures.

Lambeth Palace is the London home of the Archbishop of Canterbury, dating back to the 15th century. It contains a good collection of portraits.

St James's Palace was built by Henry VIII, although other sovereigns added to it as time went on. Originally it was built on the site of a leper hospital dedicated to St James and this is the origin of its name. Even today foreign ambassadors are still accredited to the 'Court of St James'.

Parks

London has more parks and open spaces than any other city in the world, and each one has its own special charm and character. The GLC organises a great many entertainments in them, particularly during the holidays. Details of times are published annually in the spring brochure called 'Open Air Entertainment', which you can get by writing to the **GLC Parks Department,** enclosing 7½p.

If you are a visitor to London, you might not feel like tramping round the streets and museums on a hot summer day, but you will find the Central London parks worth a visit. This section contains all those in Central London and some of the ones further out. If your favourite is not here, it is because there simply isn't enough space for them all.

Alexandra Park's grounds contain a boating lake, a pitch and putt course, a one o'clock club, and an artificial ski slope. Alexandra Palace itself houses Britain's largest indoor roller skating rink.

Battersea Park came into existence when the Royal Victoria Dock was being excavated, and the unwanted soil was dumped into a swamp on the South Bank of the river. Now, of course, it is famous for its Funfair and Festival Gardens. You can spend ages there provided your money lasts out. There is also a boating lake, a children's zoo, a play park, a one o'clock club, gardens and playing fields. During the summer there are live theatre shows for children twice daily at the concert pavilion. There are sometimes open-air exhibitions of sculpture, and recently the annual Easter Parade has taken place here instead of Hyde Park.

Blackheath, south of Greenwich Park, is a wild open common which used to be a favourite haunt of 18th century highwaymen. On the south-east corner there is a crescent of 18th century villas joined by colonnades, called the Paragon. Every Bank Holiday there is a large noisy fair.

Bushey Park, near Teddington, is famous for its mile long avenue of chestnut trees. It was planned by Christopher Wren so that there would be a magnificent approach to Hampton Court Palace. The chestnuts were planted in 1699 and there are now ten miles of lime trees as well. Each spring, when the chestnuts are likely to be in full bloom, the Superintendent of the Royal Parks fixes a date for 'Chestnut Sunday'. A large herd of deer wanders about and the ornamental ponds are filled with carp.

Crystal Palace Park and Grounds, totalling 200 acres, includes the National Sports Centre opened by the Duke of Edinburgh in 1964, and a public park with many interesting features and activities. The Crystal Palace was the great glass hall built by Joseph Paxton for the Great Exhibition of 1851 in Hyde Park. It was moved to this site in 1854 but was destroyed in a spectacular fire in 1936. The only survivals of the Exhibition are the plaster prehistoric monsters on the islands in the boating-lake at the south-west corner of this huge park. It contains a children's zoo, a play park, a one o'clock club, a large rock and water garden, an open-air concert bowl, and a floodlit artificial ski slope.

The National Sports Centre provides facilities for the training of coaches and players in almost every amateur game and sport. There is a stadium, a running track, a football pitch, a sports hall, a swimming pool and London's only motor-racing circuit. Any enquiries about these facilities should be made to the director of the centre.

Epping Forest in Essex, stretches ten miles from Chingford to the town of Epping. Although it is outside London, it is just within reach and is a good place to go for a day away from the city. Its 5,800 acres contain plenty of quiet spots where you may see a black fallow deer, a badger, fox, weasel or stoat, as well as squirrels and rabbits. Although you could get lost in the thick woods of oak, beech, birch, holly and horn-beam, there are well-known tracks that you can keep to. One of these is the Green Ride, which was cut through the woods to allow Queen Victoria to drive along when the forest was first opened to the public. You can hire a boat on Connaught Waters, and at High Beach there is a swimming pool and refreshment huts. Nearby is Dick Turpin's Cave, an inn which displays a cutlass and pistol which are supposed to have belonged to that highwayman. There are plenty of open spaces for cricket and football, and on Bank Holidays there are funfairs on Wan-stead Flats and Chingford Plain.

Green Park is a small, informal park in the centre of London. It is beautifully green in the summer and bright with crocuses and daffodils in the spring. If you have just come from the bustle and roar of the traffic at Hyde Park Corner you will find it very peaceful.

Ham Common is one of the most rural parts of London. It is on the west side of Richmond Park and close to the river—there is a pleasant walk which takes you to Ham House and the Thames towpath. You will actually see cows here, grazing on the edge of the village cricket green, and ducks in the pond. There is gorse and bracken, wild flowers and lots of trees.

Hampstead Heath consists of 200 acres of wild heathland where you can wander at will and enjoy trees, grasses, wild flowers, birds, butter-flies and pond life. You can play on the smooth slopes, ride, sail model yachts, fly kites, fish and swim in the ponds. In the winter there is a slope near Whitestone Pond which is marvellous for sledging, and people even ski on Parliament Hill. On Bank Holidays there is a fair, and there are donkey-rides at Whitestone Pond.

On the west side of Hampstead Heath is Golders Hill Park, which has an animal enclosure, a putting green, tennis courts, and a lake. On the east side are Kenwood, Highgate Ponds, and Parliament Hill. Kenwood House houses the Iveagh Bequest, a collection of furniture and paint-ings. In the summer there are open-air concerts by the lake, and the highly decorated Buckland caravan—once the home of the gypsy family of that name who came to Hampstead Heath fairs—is on show. In the Orangery there are chamber concerts and poetry readings during the summer months. Parliament Hill has a playpark, a one o'clock club and a chain of six ponds where you can swim, fish, or sail your model boat. There is also a bowling green and tennis courts.

Holland Park in Kensington has 55 acres of beautiful gardens and lawns. The house itself was bombed during the war, but the east wing has been restored and a modern youth hostel built alongside. The central section was restored in 1964 and is now an open-air theatre where plays, concerts, opera, ballet and Spanish dancing are presented in the summer. There are several formal gardens, one of them being a Dutch Garden full of tulips and bordered by an old brick wall covered with creepers. The Irish Garden has a fountain and a goldfish pool.

On the north side of the park there is a 28 acre woodland with many different varieties of trees and shrubs, where a great number of birds can be spotted.

There are football and cricket pitches, tennis courts, golf nets and a squash court. As well as this it contains a play park and a one o'clock club. During the summer children's shows are also staged in the park.

Hyde Park is the best known park in London. Its 361 acres stretch from Park Lane to Kensington, and from the Bayswater Road in the north to Knightsbridge in the South. The Serpentine has facilities for rowing, sailing, swimming at the Lido, and fishing. You can ride along Rotten Row, hire deck chairs to sit in the sun, feed the ducks, or listen to the soap-box orators at Speakers' Corner. Hyde Park is the starting point of a Veteran Car Run to Brighton, and the place where the Sheep Dog Trials take place (see under **Calendar**). It is also a popular place for pop concerts and the rallying point for demonstrations. Royal Salutes are fired in Hyde Park on special occasions, and this free show is well worth watching. The firing of these salutes takes place on the Queen's official birthday, on the anniversary of her accession, and at State openings of Parliament, as well as other occasions such as the arrival of visiting royalty or Heads of State when the forty-one guns are fired by the King's Troop of the Royal Horse Artillery.

Kensington Gardens joins Hyde Park on the Kensington side, and covers 275 acres. It has always been a favourite park of children. You can sail model boats on the Round Pond, feed the swans, visit the Pet's Cemetery or fly your kite nearby. Near the Long Water is the famous statue of Peter Pan, and over on the Bayswater Road side there is a playground with swings and see-saws, and the Elfin Oak, enclosed by railings. The oak was carved by Ivor Innes from an old stump in 1930, and it was restored in 1966 by Spike Milligan. A tiny plaque tells you that it was the work of fairies.

Kew Gardens (see under **Flowers**)

Regent's Park is roughly circular in shape. It is the largest of the Central London parks. In the north-west corner is the London Zoo (see under **Animals and Birds**), and there is an open-air theatre and Queen Mary's rose garden. There is a large lake where you can hire boats or feed the swans, a small boating pond for young children, playing fields and tennis courts. Regent's Park was once a royal hunting ground, then it was designed by Nash as a park for a house which the Prince Regent planned to build on Primrose Hill. That is why its design is more formal than other parks. On Easter Monday the annual London Harness Horse Parade is held in the Inner Circle (see under **Calendar**).

Richmond Park is a large, informal park where herds of fallow and red deer roam wild. Its 2,500 acres contain plenty of wildlife, woodland

and open spaces, rhododendron plantations, and the Pen Ponds where you can fish for tiddlers, watch the water fowl, and in winter skate on the ice. There are two public golf courses, and on the west side beautiful walks down to Ham Common. You can drive right through the park until dusk—for pedestrians it is open all the time. Near the Roehampton Gate is the White Lodge, built for George II as a hunting lodge, but now the home of the Royal Ballet School.

St James's Park is probably the prettiest of the London parks. The flower beds, trees and shrubs look lovely all the year round. Its 5 acre lake is a sanctuary for all kinds of birds. The lake is crossed by a bridge, and if you stand on this bridge you will have a marvellous view of Whitehall southwards, and of Buckingham Palace to the north. Birdcage Walk, which gets its name from the aviary which was built there by Charles II, runs down one side, and the Mall down the other. The Mall also takes its name from the time of Charles II: the game 'paille-maille' used to be played there.

Waterlow Park in Highgate is famous for its aviary and ponds with different varieties of waterfowl. It is an attractive place of 26 acres presented in 1889 by Sir Sydney Waterlow whose statue, firmly grasping a stone umbrella, looks out over the park. Nell Gwynne lived in Lauderdale House within the park, and the poet Andrew Marvell spent many years in the cottage that once stood nearby.

Wimbledon Common is a thousand acres of heathland and silver-birch woodlands. It was once a popular haunt of highwaymen, and there was a gibbet at the cross-roads. There is a windmill, not open to visit, and three lakes where you can sail model boats in summer and skate in winter.

South-East London Parks

Many people don't know about the attractive woodlands and parks in the Lewisham and Blackheath area. You could spend two or three days exploring them, there is plenty to see and do. There are two main tracts—the woodlands on Shooters Hill, and two-mile long belt formed by Bostall Heath and Woods and Lesnes Abbey Woods. Shooters Hill woodlands consist of Eltham Common; Castlewood, where you can see Severndroog Castle, built in 1784 by Sir William James to commemorate his exploits against the pirates of the Malabar Coast of India; Jackwood; Oxleas Woods, where you can ride horses; and Eltham Park, where there are open air swimming baths, putting greens and tennis courts.

In Lesnes Abbey Woods you can see the remains of the Abbey which was built nearly eight hundred years ago in the reign of Henry II. If you go in the spring you will see 20 acres of wild daffodils, and other woodland flowers. Bostall Heath has a bowling green, and provides wonderful views over south-east London. Smaller parks in this area are Shrewsbury Park; Eaglesfield, where there are two pens, one with red deer and one with Exmoor ponies; Charlton Park, which has a play park and a one o'clock club, and also a putting green and tennis courts; Maryon Park, which has a putting green; and Hornfair, which has an open-air lido, a bowling green, and tennis courts.

Parties

Just in case you get asked to a fancy-dress party and feel rich enough to hire a costume, or if you are giving a party and want to buy jokes and balloons or even hire a film, these are the places to go to:

B.B. Film Services, 24 Worcester Crescent, Mill Hill, NW7, Tel: 959 2937 have a good selection.

Barnum (Carnival Novelties) Ltd., 67 Hammersmith Road, W14, Tel: 602 1211 for costumes, masks, jokes, balloons and everything else.

Kensington Carnival Co., 123 Ifield Road, SW10, Tel: 370 4358 for party novelties.

M. Berman, 30 Rupert Street, W1, Tel: 839 1651 for costumes.

Magic Shop, 12 Oxford Street, W1, Tel: 636 8752 for magic and jokes.

Lewis Davenport, 51 Great Russell Street, WC1, Tel: 405 8524 for magic and jokes.

Nathan's, 141 Drury Lane, WC2, Tel: 836 3150 for costumes.

Party Film Shows, 1 Riders Terrace, NW8, Tel: 624 5333 give a Tot's Fun Show with fairy stories and puppetoons from £5.50. Shows for older people are from £6.35.

The Theatre Zoo, 28 New Row, WC2, Tel: 836 3150 for animal costumes, hideous masks and fake noses.

Wallace Heaton, 127 New Bond Street, W1, Tel: 629 7511 has films for parties—cartoons, silent movies, comedies, Westerns etc.

Planetariums

There are two planetariums in the London area, the London Planetarium and the one at Greenwich.

London Planetarium is next to Madame Tussaud's in Baker Street and you can visit both of them on a joint ticket costing 35p (adults 75p). An enormous Zeiss projector throws a realistic reproduction of the ever-changing night sky as seen from any point on the earth's surface on to the hemispherical ceiling of the auditorium. New presentation every hour, varying from a visit to the polar regions to the exploration of space.

Greenwich Planetarium is open to the public only on Saturdays during term-time. During the week it is reserved for school parties. During the holidays there are often special talks for children of 9 years up on the stars and the sun.

In Greenwich Park are the Old Royal Observatory buildings. The

Royal Observatory is now at Herstmonceux. The buildings now belong to the National Maritime Museum and are devoted to exhibitions of astronomy and navigation. Flamstead House, the oldest part, is used to exhibit astronomical instruments, some of them used in the Old Observatory. The Planetarium is in one of the other buildings. The Greenwich Meridian, from which we measure Greenwich Mean Time, runs across the courtyard, and you can actually straddle it if you want to.

Play Parks

Play parks are for children from five years up to school leaving age. They are open from Easter until September, from 17.30 to 20.00 during term time, and from 9.30 to 18.00 or 20.00 during school holidays. On Saturdays and Sundays they are open from 13.30 to 18.00. Play parks offer a wide range of activities such as climbing, digging, building tree houses, rope railways, climbing and balancing apparatus, drama, painting, modelling, table tennis and other games, and all sorts of handicrafts. Each playpark is developed individually under the leadership of trained staff, but all of them have the same friendly and informal atmosphere. At the moment there are play parks in the following parks, but check with **GLC Parks Department** for up-to-date information.

Bartlett Park, Arcadia Street, Poplar, E14
Battersea Park, The Sun Gate, Albert Bridge Road, SW11
Beckenham Place Park, Old Bromley Road, SE6
Brockwell Park, Arlington Road, Tulse Hill, SW2
Charlton Park, Charlton Park Road, SE7
Clissold Park, Green Lanes, N4
Crystal Palace Park, Crystal Palace Park Road, SE19
Deptford Park, New King Street, SE8
Geraldine Mary Harmsworth Park, St George's Road, SE1
Hackney Marsh, Daubeney Road, Homerton, E9
Haggerston Park, Edith Street, Shoreditch, E2
Holland Park, Kensington High Street, W8
Kennington Park, St Agnes Place, Kennington Park Road, SE11
Kensington Memorial Park, St Mark's Road, W10
Little Wormwood Scrubs, Dalgarno Gardens, W10
Margaret McMillan Park, Watson's Street, New Cross, SE8
Millwall Park, Douglas Place, Manchester Road, Cubitt Town, E14
Parliament Hill, Highgate Road, Kentish Town, NW5
Patmore Estate, Thessaly Road, SW8
Peckham Rye Park, junction of Peckham Rye and Homestall Road, SE22
Ravenscourt Park, Paddenswick Road, Hammersmith, W6
Slade Garden, Robsart Street, North Brixton, SW9
Southwark Park, Southwark Park Road, Rotherhithe, SE16

Springfield Park, Springfield off Upper Clapton Road, E5
Telegraph Hill, Pepys Road, off Kitto Road, New Cross, SE14
Victoria Park, Approach Road, Hackney, E2
Wandsworth Common, Bolingbroke Grove, SW11
Wapping Gardens, Greenbank, Wapping, E1
(Bartlett Park, Deptford Park and Hackney Marsh are open all the year.)

Politics

Traditionally, the best place to hear people saying exactly what they like about anything under the sun, is **Speaker's Corner** in Hyde Park. The other places where you will get the same kind of free entertainment are **Tower Hill** and **Lincoln's Inn Fields.**

Although there are frequently demonstrations going on in London, we have very few traditional marches. The only march as such is the May Day Procession organised by the Labour Party. The Conservative Party have their own ceremony on Primrose Day when a small group of people lay primroses at the foot of the statue of Lord Beaconsfield in Parliament Square. A small ceremony takes place at Karl Marx's grave in Highgate on the anniversary of his death.

If you want to belong to or just find out about political parties, get in touch with the central offices of the organisations below. Minority groups have not been included but if you want to find out about them buy a guide like 'Alternative London'.

Communist Party of Great Britain (Marxist-Leninist), 155 Fortress Road, NW5
Labour Party Youth Officer, Transport House, Smith Square, SW1, Tel: 834 9434
National League of Young Liberals, 69 Blackfriars Road, SE1, Tel: 928 2883

National Union of Students, 3 Endsleigh Street, WC1, Tel: 387 1277
Schools' Action Union, 9 Beechcroft Avenue, NW11
Socialist Party of Great Britain, 52 Clapham High Street, SW4, Tel: 622 3811
Young Communist League, National Committee, 16 King Street, London, WC2, Tel: 240 2810
Young Conservative Party and Unionist Organisation, 32 Smith Square, SW1, Tel: 222 9000

Posters

Some people simply use posters to brighten up their rooms and others collect them seriously.

MUSEUMS

British Transport Museum has a really absorbing collection.

Imperial War Museum has a lot exhorting people to do their bit for their country during the last two wars.

London Museum has a fascinating collection which illustrates all sorts of facets of everyday life.

Victoria and Albert Museum's collection is so good that you can trace the history and development of poster design.

SHOPS

Andrew Block, 20 Barter Street, High Holborn, WC1, Tel: 405 9660 has thousands of theatrical posters.

Hang-Up Poster Shop, 43 Camden Passage, N1, Tel: 359 0183 has a huge range of contemporary posters from all over the world.

London Transport, 280 Marylebone Road, NW1, Tel: 262 3444 is rightly famous for its posters. They have some of the best designed ones today and they are all on sale from 50p-80p each. It is worth noting that this is open from 9.00-16.30 (Fridays 16.00).

Pottery

This section is intended for the serious enthusiast as well as those who just want to do a bit of potting on Saturday morning. As well as telling you where to get lessons, there is a list of museums where you can go to study ceramics of the past. For other places see under **Youth Centres, Adventure Playgrounds** and **Art and Craft** centres.

CLUBS AND CENTRES

Camden Arts Centre has lessons on Saturday and Sunday mornings for younger children, and on Saturday afternoon for teenagers. The lessons are not cheap—£9.50 for a full year of thirty weeks—but the tuition is very good.

Chelsea Pottery has lessons on Saturday. You pay a yearly membership fee, and then individually for each 2 hour lesson. If a whole family joins, family membership works out cheaper.

Miss Meyer-Michael gives small, private tuition classes for children in Hampstead, particularly during the school holidays.

Moonrock now has a pottery school at the home of one of the leaders.

Theatre Centre, NW10, is open on Wednesdays and includes pottery lessons.

PLACES TO SEE POTTERY

Bethnal Green Museum has a collection of domestic pottery and porcelain, showing its development from the 16th century.

British Museum has many examples in the antiquities section of British, Medieval, Greek, Roman and Oriental Ceramics. The famous Portland Vase is exhibited here.

The Craft Centre has exhibitions of pottery by today's young potters.

London Museum has a small but good collection of 15th, 16th and 17th century pottery, including a great deal from the London Potteries.

Pottery Lane, near Holland Park, used to be famous for brick making and pottery in Victorian days. At the end of the lane you can still see an old pottery kiln. Some of the pots made there are now exhibited in the London Museum.

Martinware Pottery Collection. There is a large collection of Martinware including face mugs, birds, grotesques, and other delightful pieces.

Percival David Foundation has a marvellous collection of Chinese Porcelain—Sung Dynasty, Ming and Ch'ing.

Old Battersea House, in Putney, originally the home of William de Morgan, is now a museum housing the De Morgan pottery.

Sir John Soane's Museum has a small collection of Wedgewood, and the famous Cawdor vase.

Victoria and Albert Museum. The collection includes ceramics from the first to the 19th century from the West to the Orient. There is also the Schreiber collection of English ceramics.

Wallace Collection has an outstanding collection of French 17th and 18th century ceramics.

William Morris Gallery has a collection of vases, tiles and dishes.

SHOPS

The best place to buy all the materials you need is the **Fulham Pottery,** 210 New Kings Road, SW6, Tel: 736 1188 who will send you a catalogue on request.

If you want to see or buy modern pottery, some of the best places are **The Craft Centre**, 43 Earlham Street, WC2, Tel: 240 3327; **The Craftsman Potters Shop,** Marshall Street, W1, Tel: 437 7605; and **Heal's,** 196 Tottenham Court Road, W1, Tel: 580 3781.

MAGAZINES

'Ceramics'; 'Pottery Quarterly'.

Pre-School Playgroups

Playgroups are for children of 3-5 years. Their aim is to widen the scope of the young child's life and to let him get used to mixing with other children at a young age. They also help to break down the isolation of young mothers, and to help them understand the needs of their children. Playgroups lasting about 2½ hours are usually held two or three times a week. Activities include painting, drawing, plasticine, story-time, sand-pits, etc.

There are hundreds of playgroups all over London. To find out whether there is one near you, get in touch with the **Pre-School Playgroups Association**. The groups are normally held in church halls, community centres or private homes.

Mothers can join the Association for £1.50 a year, and will receive ten editions of the magazine 'Contact'. Other publications are 'Playgroup Activities' and 'How to Start a Playgroup'.

Puppets

The art of puppetry is one that has never died out and there has been a revival of interest in it during the past few years. A number of children's workshops and craft centres such as the **Curtain Theatre** and the **Unicorn Theatre** have classes in this old art.

Perhaps the best known puppet theatre is the **Little Angel Marionette Theatre** which is open at weekends and throughout school holidays. It puts on two performances a day, one for those under 6 and the other for those who are over 6.

Puppet shows are often put on in the **Concert Pavilion** at **Battersea Park** during the summer holidays.

The **Educational Puppetry Association** is a very helpful organisation which meets on Monday evenings at 18.30 and produces a magazine and newsletter. Other classes run by the ILEA are mentioned in 'Floodlight'.

Riding

If you want to ride, there are riding schools right in the centre of London. Rotten Row in Hyde Park is a popular place for riders. The **Greater London Horseman's Association,** 74 High Street, Teddington, Middlesex, will give advice to anyone who wants to know about riding in London. A selection of riding schools are given below. Prices vary, but £1 an hour is about average, although it may be as high as £1.50 in Central London. **The Pony Club** will also provide a list of recommended schools.

RIDING SCHOOLS
Lilo Blum, 32a Grosvenor Crescent Mews, SW1, Tel: 235 6846
Childs Hill Riding School, The Mews, Devonshire Place, NW7, Tel: 435 6130

Dulwich Riding School, Dulwich Common, SE21, Tel: 693 2944
The Equestrian Centre, The Ridgeway, Mill Hill, NW7, Tel: 959 3818
Estelle Stables, 63 Bathurst Mews, W2, Tel: 723 2813
Frith Manor Stables, Lullington Garth, N12, Tel: 346 6703
Hilcote Riding School, 25b High Street, Wimbledon, SW19, Tel: 946 2520
Knightsbridge Riding School Ltd., 11 Elveston Mews, SW7, Tel: 584 8474
Lester Riding Establishment, Roehampton, High Street, SW15, Tel: 788 6070
Mottingham Riding School, Mottingham Lane, SE9, Tel: 857 3003
Queen Elizabeth Riding School, 97 Forest Side, Chingford, E4, Tel: 529 1223
South London School of Equitation, 117a Canterbury Grove, SE27, Tel: 670 0775

SHOPS
One of the best ways to get equipped is to buy second-hand clothes but if you can afford new go to:
Moss Bros, Covent Garden, WC2, Tel: 240 4567 sell both new and second-hand riding equipment for children.
Rowes, 120 New Bond Street, W1, Tel: 629 3941 sell top quality riding clothes for children.

SHOWS AND EXHIBITIONS
Greater London Horse Show (Clapham Common); **Horse of the Year Show** (Wembley in October); **International Horse Show** (the White City in July); and just out of London, **Richmond Royal Horse Show** (Ascot Heath, June); **Royal Windsor Horse Show** (Home Park, Windsor, May).

Rugby Football

It is curious that rugby all seems to happen in a small corner of London round about Richmond and Twickenham.
For information about games, beginners' courses, coaching and training

ask the **Rugby Football Union** who are always ready to give help and advice.

There are games in the following **GLC Parks: Battersea; Hainault Forest, North Camberwell Open Space** and **Wormwood Scrubs.**

Apart from the great rugby occasions one of the best things to go and see if you are not really very knowledgeable is the Middlesex Seven-a-Side competition held towards the end of April. It goes on for the whole day and the spectators become almost as tired as the players.

Science

Anyone who is interested in science should join the **British Association of Young Scientists**, which was started in 1968 and has a number of branches in the London area. It is open to anyone from 12-18, and membership is only 25p a year. Each branch organises its own events—lectures, films, visits etc, and in addition the Head Office at 20 Great Smith Street, SW1, Tel: 799 7657 organises special lectures once a year in January or February at their headquarters.

Every year there is a course of special programmes lasting a week, usually in September. This necessitates going away to stay for a week in Leicester. There are a certain number of bursaries which are awarded to BAYS members who have been on summer courses, either at home or abroad. The Association produces a magazine, 'Forum', which is sent to all members.

For details of membership write to the Secretary of Head Office, who will tell you where your nearest branch is.

MUSEUMS
Flamstead House, Greenwich Park, has a collection of astrological instruments, sundials, sandglasses, astrolobes etc.

Gordon Medical Museum is the place to go if you are interested in medical science and diseases in humans. The museum is intended for serious students only. Write to the Dean of the Medical School or the Curator for permission to visit.

Health Exhibition Centre has a permanent exhibition of modern public health subjects and occasional special exhibitions.

Industrial Health and Safety Centre has a permanent exhibition of methods of promoting the health and safety of industrial workers.

National Maritime Museum has exhibitions of nautical instruments and navigational aids. During the school holidays there are special events for children. At Christmas there are lectures, at Easter films, and during the Summer lectures and films.

Pharmaceutical Society's Museum is for serious students only; arrange with the Curator before you visit. The museum has a vast collection of crude drugs used in the 17th century; early printed works, manuscripts and prints relating to pharmacy; English delft drug jars, leech jars, medicine chests, dispensing apparatus etc.

Science Museum has historical collections dealing with maths, physics, chemistry, engineering, transport, communications, mining, industry etc from early times to the present day. Among the newest acquisitions are the space suit worn by Captain Anders to circle the moon, and four minute pieces of the Moon itself. There are many working models and scale models, and an Illumination Gallery. The Children's Gallery in the basement has lots of fascinating models that you can work yourself. There are films for children from Monday to Saturday at 12.30. There are also scientific films, not specifically for children, but they can watch as well, at 13.00 on Tuesday, Thursday and Saturday. A programme of the month's films and lectures is available free on request.

St Thomas's Operating Theatre is fascinating because it is a 19th century building complete with the instruments of the time and showing the conditions under which surgeons worked and patients suffered.

Wellcome Institute of the History of Medicine has collections which illustrate the history of medicine and allied sciences from earliest times to the present century. Selected material and special exhibitions are open to the public.

SHOPS

You can often pick up old scientific instruments or bits of them in the markets. There are some excellent stalls in the Portobello Road.

Proops, 52 Tottenham Court Road, W1, Tel: 580 0141, has all sorts of science hobby equipment such as small hydraulic devices, valves, pumps, motors, aircraft indicators, tachometers, sensing devices etc.

LECTURES

During the school holidays, particularly at Christmas, many scientific organisations give lectures specially for young people. These are usually advertised in the national press. The following are the type of bodies who might organise such events: **Institute of Fuel; Institution of Civil Engineers; Institution of Structural Engineers; Royal Aeronautical Society; Royal College of Surgeons; Royal Institution of Great Britain; Royal Society of Medicine.**

MAGAZINES

There are many magazines on scientific subjects, too numerous to mention here. Find a good newsagent and ask what is available on your particular interest.

Signs

There are, of course, so many street signs that it is impossible to list them all, but while you are wandering round London you might spot the following ones.

Billingsgate has golden fish weather vanes.

City of London lamp-posts have different signs. Some of them carry a shield and red dagger, part of the arms of the city, others have signs to indicate what parish you are in.

Over the premises of Davison, Newman & Co. Ltd. in **Creechurch Lane** is a sign consisting of three lumps of sugar with a crown above them and the date of 1650.

In the **Cuming Museum** is the 'Dog and Pot' shop sign.

Fish Street Hill has a carved sign outside a rope-maker's shop showing two men in a double-ended boat (a peterboat) with one man casting a net while the other is fishing.

Guildhall Museum has pilgrim signs and badges as well as shop and tavern signs.

Lombard Street has a great number of hanging signs.

Every lamp-post down the **Mall** has a small 14th century ship with a square sail on top of it.

A **golden grasshopper**, 11 feet long, is to be seen on the top of the **Royal Exchange**. This was the family crest of the founder, Sir Thomas Gresham.

There are two silver **griffins** on top of posts marking the boundary of the City of London in **Holborn**. Two more griffins made of cast-iron are now in the **Temple Gardens**. They used to be on the old Coal Exchange and also marked the City boundary.

On top of the **Old Bailey**, really called the Central Criminal Court, is Justice holding a sword and scales.

Red Indian heads can be seen over the windows of 14 **Princes Gate**. This was once the official home of the USA Ambassador to Britain.

Russell Square has a notice forbidding you to take cattle, sheep, goats or pigs into the gardens.

St Clement Danes has a weather-vane with an anchor incorporated into the design. This is because St Clement is the patron saint of sailors. The Vicarage is actually called the Anchorage. You will also see this sign set into the pavement in front of Child's Bank in **Fleet Street**.

St Lawrence Jewry has, on top of the classical tower and spire, a weather vane in the shape of a gridiron, in memory of the death of this saint.

St Mary-le-Bow has a spire on top of the superb campanile, with a griffin for a weather vane.

St Nicholas Cole Abbey has a weather vane in the shape of a sailing ship on top of its tower.

Trafalgar Square has the Standard Yard (a length of bronze) built into the north wall of the fountains enclosure.

Skating

The Pen Ponds in Richmond Park, as well as the lakes in other London parks, are well-known rendezvous for skaters when the weather is cold enough for the ice to be thick. But you can hardly wait for that. If you want to skate all the year round go the the following rinks:

Queen's Ice Skating Club, Queensway, W2, Tel: 229 0172 is open 7 days a week, 3 sessions a day: 10.00-12.00; 14.00-17.00; 19.00-22.00. Membership is 15p, and you can hire skates for 10p. Tuition is available at about 50p for 15 minutes.

Richmond Ice Rink, Clevedon Road East, Twickenham, Tel: 892 3646 is open 7 days a week, 3 sessions a day: 10.00-12.30; 14.30-17.00; 19.00-22.00. There are special classes for children on Saturdays from 9.00 to 10.00, followed by free skating until 12.30. Toddlers (2-5 years) on Mondays, 15.45-16.45. Admission is 25p and you can hire skates for 10p. Tuition 40p.

Silver Blades Ice Rink, Streatham High Road, SW16, Tel: 769 7861 is open 7 days a week; 3 sessions a day: 10.00-12.15; 14.15-17.00; 19.30-22.30. There are special children's and beginners' classes. Admission is 12½p (adults 17p) and you can hire skates for 10p.

ROLLER SKATING

Britain's largest roller skating rink is at **Alexandra Palace**. It is open Monday-Saturday from 19.30 to 22.30, and there are special children's sessions on Saturday mornings 10.30-12.30. Admission is 15p, and you can hire roller skates for 15p.

Ski-ing

You don't need snow to get in training for your winter ski-ing holiday. There are several artificial ski slopes in London that offer pre-ski tuition. When it *does* snow, though, you can get the real thing on Parliament Hill, Hampstead Heath. There are often a few keen skiers who will give you cheap lessons.

Crystal Palace Sports Centre has a floodlit artificial ski-slope which is open from October to April. There is a nursery slope for beginners and an area where more experienced skiers can practise. Beginners' courses are usually three 2-hour sessions, and cost from £3.60. Moderate skiers' courses cost £4.50. More experienced skiers pay 70p an hour. All charges include instruction, hire of boots, skis and sticks, and showers and changing facilities. You must be a member of the Centre first. Annual membership is 50p (adults £1).

The GLC also provides the largest (1,000 square yards of ski mat) outdoor ski slope in England at **Alexandra Palace** and offers courses for beginners as well as advanced skiers. Practice runs cost only £1.25 for 2 hours. There is a toboggan run for those who prefer it.

There are also pre-ski training slopes which give lessons for children at **Philbeach Hall**, Philbeach Gardens, SW5, Tel: 373 8898 and **Simpsons,** 203 Piccadilly, W1, Tel: 734 2002. At both places there are private lessons every afternoon on weekdays and on Saturday mornings. One lesson of 40 minutes costs £3.00 for the first child, and 25p for each additional child at the same lesson. At Philbeach Hall children can go along to the public lessons from 17.00 to 22.00, every evening. Six lessons of one hour cost £6.00, and there are 10 people at each lesson. Both ski slopes are open from November to the end of March.

At **Parliament Hill Fields** you can have fun ski-ing on grass in the summer on the special skis-cum-roller skates at £1 a session. These sessions are held on Saturday and Sunday afternoons from 14.00 onwards. A lift takes you back to the top after each downhill run.

SHOPS
Lillywhites, Piccadilly Circus, SW1, Tel: 930 3181 and **Pindisports,** 14-18 Holborn, EC1, Tel: 242 3278 sell ski-ing equipment and clothes for children. If you don't want to buy, you can hire children's ski equipment from **Moss Bros,** Covent Garden, WC2, Tel: 240 4567. Sample costs for 15 days are £2.45 for a jacket, £3.20 for trousers, £2.35 for lace-up boots.

Stamps

There are numerous shops, exhibitions, clubs, books and magazines, and museums for stamps in London.

MUSEUMS
British Museum has a remarkable collection of stamps.
National Postal Museum has a splendid collection which traces the history of the British postage stamp. Special lectures are given in the holidays for people who are still at school or interested in stamps. Details of the times are given in the national press and in stamp magazines. .
Tottenham Museum, Bruce Castle, also has a good collection of stamps.

FIRST DAY COVERS

Philatelic Bureau of the GPO will, for a deposit, send them to you. Central London post offices like Trafalgar Square provide a special post box where 'First Day of Issue' will be stamped on covers. Many stamp dealers including those listed below, sell their own first day covers.

Argyll Stamp Company, 265 Strand, WC2, Tel: 242 3688

B and M Stamps, 3 Hurst Avenue, Chingford, E4 (This is not a shop; it is a postal service only.)

Historic Relics, 95 Cranbourne Road, SW12, Tel: 673 5262

Philart Productions, 11 Bermondsey Street, SE1, Tel: 407 0710

STAMP AUCTIONS

City of London Philatelic Auctions, 170 Bishopsgate, EC2, Tel: 283 7968

Stanley Gibbons, 391 Strand, WC2, Tel: 836 9707

H.R. Harmer, 41 New Bond Street, W1, Tel: 629 0218

London Stamp Exchange, 5 Buckingham Street, WC2, Tel: 930 1413

Plumridge & Co, 142 Strand, WC2, Tel: 836 0939

DEALERS

Bridger & Kay, 86 Strand, WC2, Tel: 836 3216 deal in British Colonial and Commonwealth stamps from Queen Victoria to today.

Eric Etkin, 23 Cranbourne Street, WC2, Tel: 240 2822 deals in general stamps of the world.

David Field, 42 Berkeley Street, W1, Tel: 499 5252 deals in British and Commonwealth stamps.

Stanley Gibbons, 391 Strand, WC2, Tel: 836 9707 has the best and most comprehensive collection in London. These include stamps from every country in the world, from the rarest to new issues. Here you can buy stamp albums, accessories and, of course, the famous catalogue.

Metropolitan Stamps, 327 Edgware Road, W2, Tel: 723 3893 are retail and wholesale dealers in all kinds of stamps.

Strand Stamp Centre, 84 Strand, WC2, Tel: 836 5011 deals in every sort of stamp.

H.A. Wallace, 94 Old Broad Street, EC2, Tel: 588 5306 deals in classic issues of Great Britain and the Commonwealth.

C. Zinopoulos, 34 St. Martin's Court, WC2, Tel: 836 3800 has a world-wide collection but specializes in Greek stamps.

SHOWS AND EXHIBITIONS

Stamp exhibitions are usually advertised in all philatelist magazines, or you can get details from the **Philatelic Traders Society.**

Philympia, the great international stamp exhibition, is held every ten years at **Olympia.** You will have to wait until 1980 for the next one.

Stampex is the annual fair held in the first week of March at the **Royal Horticultural Society's Hall.** This is for British dealers only.

SOCIETIES

National Philatelic Society is open to anyone over the age of 16 who is interested in stamps. A magazine is published every fortnight, and a meeting is held once a month. The committee answers members' queries.

MAGAZINES
There are a number of these: 'Gibbons Stamp Monthly'; 'Philatelic Magazine'; 'The Philatelist'; 'Philately'; 'Stamp Collecting'; 'Stamp Lovers'; 'The Stamp Magazine'; 'Stamp Weekly'.

Swimming

There are so many indoor pools it is impossible to list them all but visitors to London who fancy a swim really should try the baths at Swiss Cottage, the Oasis in Endell Street, and the National Sports Centre at the Crystal Palace. For hardy outdoor swimmers it is worth knowing that entry is free at all outdoor pools provided you get there and are swimming before 7.00. As long as you are already there you can stay for free for the rest of the session.

OPEN-AIR POOLS:
Brockwell Park Lido, SE24, Tel: 274 7991
Eltham Park South Baths, SE9, Tel: 850 2031
Geraldine Mary Harmsworth Children's Lido, Harmsworth Park, SE1, Tel: 735 3074
Highbury Fields Baths, N5, Tel: 226 2334
Highgate Ponds, N6, (men only)
Hornfair Baths, SE7, Tel: 854 2575
Kennington Park Baths, SE11, Tel: 735 2216
Kenwood Pond, N6, Tel: 340 5303 (women only)
London Fields Baths, E8, Tel: 254 6947
Parliament Hill Lido, NW5, Tel: 485 3873
Peckham Rye Park Baths, SE22, Tel: 693 3791
Serpentine Lido, Hyde Park, SW7
Southwark Park Baths, SE16, Tel: 237 2717
Tooting Common Baths, SW17, Tel: 769 4226
Victoria Park Lido, E2, Tel: 985 6774
Wimbledon Common, SW19, Tel: 788 7655 (men only)

LESSONS
Amateur Swimming Association is the body you can go to to find out about clubs, coaching and tests.

SUB-AQUA SWIMMING
British Sub-Aqua Club is an organisation for people interested in under-water swimming, snorkelling, spear-fishing and underwater exploration. They also organise holdiays both at home and abroad. They have a junior section for people who are under 15. Do not think that sub-

103

aqua swimming is something you can just pick up. It's terribly dangerous unless you have been properly trained.

Ten-Pin Bowling

Ten Pin Bowling rushed in on London like a lion and although it hasn't quite gone out like a lamb, the number of places where you can have a game is much smaller than it was a couple of years ago.

ABC Cine Bowl, Broadway, Bexleyheath, Tel: 303 3325
ABC Leytonstone High Road, E11, Tel: 539 2309
Airport Bowl, Bath Road, Harlington, Tel: 759 1396
Mecca, 142 Streatham Hill, SW16, Tel: 674 5251
Piccadilly Bowl, 30 Shaftesbury Avenue, W1, Tel: 437 1580
Wembley Stadium Bowl, Empire Stadium, Wembley, Tel: 902 8560

Most of these start their sessions round about 10.00 and stay open until late in the evening.

If you become really keen the organisation to get in touch with is the **British Ten Pin Bowling Association.**

Television

You can get free tickets for TV and radio audience shows by writing to the Ticket Office well in advance. If you want to be in the audience of a particular show you may have to wait some time. If you are not fussy, but just want to be on *something,* tell them how old you are and what sort of programme you like, and you might get tickets quicker.

ATV Studio, Boreham Wood, Herts
BBC Ticket Unit, 16 Langham Street, London W1A 1AA, for radio and TV shows. The TV shows take place mostly at the Television Centre, Shepherds Bush, and you must be over 14, except for programmes like 'Crackerjack' and 'Basil Brush'.
Granada TV Network Ltd, Studio Ten, Kings Road, SW3
London Weekend, Station House, Harrow Road, Wembley, Middlesex, offers tickets to people over 15 only.

Rediffusion Limited, Television House, Kingsway, WC2.
Thames Television, Television House, 306 Euston Road, NW1, actually records mainly at Elstree and Teddington.

TELEVISION GALLERY (see **Conducted Tours**)

Tennis

Many of the London parks such as **Regent's Park, Battersea Park, Waterlow Park** and **Lincoln's Inn Fields** have hard courts open throughout the year. If you become a registered player, which is quite cheap, you can hire a court in advance. If you are not registered it costs a little more and you have to take your chance if you turn up hoping for a game. The **GLC Parks Department** produces a leaflet which you can write for.

If you want to play on a local Borough court get details from the Town Hall or the local library.

COACHING
CCPR offers information regarding coaching.
GLC runs a coaching scheme at some parks. Write for details.
Lawn Tennis Association offers advice and information. If you want to be coached or to join a club they are the people to get in touch with.

WATCHING
All-England Lawn Tennis Championships—Wimbledon Fortnight—begins towards the end of June. The Centre Court holds 15,000 and it's always packed. It's worth going just for the atmosphere.
GLC Championships are held at Queen's Club in August.
Junior Covered Court Championship is held in January at Queen's Club.
London Hard Courts Championships are held at Hurlingham in April.
National Covered Court Championships are held in February at Queen's Club.
Queen's Club Championship held in June is the overture to Wimbledon. All the great names are there, warming up for the biggest tennis occasion in the world.

Theatre

If you simply want to be part of an audience watching plays, that's fine. There are always good shows, and the gallery of most theatres is still very cheap. If, however, you want to take a more active part, that's even better. The opportunities to become involved are growing all the time.

There are a number of theatre workshops about—multimedia places —and these no longer believe in the separation of different branches of the arts and so at many of them you can take part in film-making, music, poetry, dance, drama, puppetry, crafts and painting, light shows and other things. The cost is low, the people running them usually young and enthusiastic. Belonging to one of the art workshops has other advantages because they frequently have arrangements with other organisations, so that you can get cheap theatre and concert seats and so on.

The following list will give you some idea of what is available:

Children's Theatre Workshop operates on Saturdays from 9.30-12.30. Small groups are formed for improvisation, arts and crafts and so on. They aim to put on productions in theatres and have already produced *Tom Sawyer*.

Cockpit Theatre and Arts Workshop in Marylebone is a fantastic place which incorporates performances, exhibitions, music (folk and jazz), film-making, environmental events, festivals (especially during the summer), exploration into other arts media and poetry. This is cheap. It costs 25p a term; group membership is £1 a year or 40p a term.

There is a coffee bar, one main course is served at lunchtime and in the early evening, and often, at lunchtime, there is some sort of entertainment too.

Group 64 Youth Theatre Workshop in Putney operates from a converted church. It is for people of 15-25 and welcomes unskilled enthusiasts (they can always find something for them to do). Group 64 aims to put on a play once a month. As well as this they have other activities related to the arts and there is a good folk club on Sunday evening.

Inter-Action is in a section on its own.

Moonrock, at the moment having some difficulty in finding a permanent home, offers an astonishingly varied programme including light shows, painting, modelling, pop, dance and drama. This usually functions on Saturday mornings from 10.00-13.00, is for people from 4-12 years and costs about 5p a visit.

Oval House is another very alive multimedia place. Intended for those between 15-25, it offers jazz, dance, drama, graphics, a writer's workshop, folk, socio-drama, photography and film-making as well as other activities.

If you become a full member at £2.10 a year you can take part in everything going on. For 50p a year you can join the Theatre Club—and this means anyone of any age—where you can watch and become involved in the performances. The Club is open every evening from 19.30-23.30 and all day long on Saturdays and Sundays.

Second Centre is a specialised theatre workshop since it is meant particularly for those who are thinking of making a career in the theatre and want to know what it is all about. It is meant too, for those involved in forms of art who think that a knowledge of theatre will help. There are twice-weekly sessions. For further information write to the Director.

South London Theatre Centre in South Norwood operates from a converted fire station. Although it is basically a repertory company, a lot of other things like photography, sewing, painting and music go on there. Classes are held in stage design and lighting as well as a dance drama and acting courses. It puts on a play about once a month and welcomes anyone over 15.

This centre is open every evening from 19.30-23.00 (including Sundays). The membership for a year is £3 but for 50p a year you can buy tickets to performances at very reasonable prices.

Theatre Centre has companies which visit schools and clubs but at the same time it operates sessions on Wednesdays (16.30-18.00 for 9-11 years; 19.00-21.00 for 11-13 years; Saturday mornings for 5-10 years). At these sessions which cost only 5p (it is free the first visit) you can do pottery, sculpture, painting, drama, film-making and other activities.

Young People's Theatre in Plumstead, attached to the Greenwich Theatre, has drama and art for people over the age of 7, and everyone is welcome whether they think they have talent or not. Their premises, still being worked on, are in a converted church.

THEATRE CLUBS

The Act Inn is not exactly a club. It is an organisation that aims at putting on performances daily during the holidays. The action takes place both on the stage and amongst the audience so that you might well find yourself involved in it.

Anna Scher Children's Theatre in the Essex Road operates at different times for different age groups. It is a good and cheap place (10p a class or £2 a term). If your parents happen to be really hard up because your father is out of work, don't let it put you off. They make and break their own rules about money very happily. Junior classes for those between 6-11 are on Tuesday and Thursday. Senior classes, 11-16, on Monday and Wednesday. During the holidays plays you have been rehearsing during the term are put on.

British Drama League run Junior Drama League holiday courses. For more information apply to the Organiser.

Curtain Theatre Club does have an age limit. It is primarily a club for people up to the age of 12. Many activities connected with the theatre go on here, particularly on Saturdays 10.30-12.30 (3p a week). Short courses are held for people of 14 upwards. For more details, get in touch with the Manager.

Minerva Youth Theatre does not yet have a permanent home of its own. They hope that their members will take part in everything—from painting to making props. The age range for this group is 16-25.

Mountview Theatre Club is a good amateur club with a very high standard. They welcome younger members.

National Youth Theatre puts on plays with young people in them at very reasonable prices. Now it has a permanent home in the Shaw Theatre they will become increasingly active. They already run courses, put on demonstrations, jazz and pop sessions and poetry readings. If you hope to become a member of the company itself (age range 14-21) write for details of auditions.

Questors Theatre in Ealing is a very good amateur theatre with extremely high standards. They run 8 regular weekly groups for young people including an under 14 junior theatre workshop on Saturday afternoons. If you are under 18 the cost of membership is £1 and for that, apart from being able to go there to take part in activities, you can see 10 shows for free.

Unicorn Theatre for Young People is a very well-established club for people from 4-18. Apart from performances given in the theatre—and these very often include specially written plays—there is a very well-equipped theatre workshop and improvisation sessions, usually held on Saturday mornings. An improvisation session costs about 65p and includes a drink in the morning and lunch. Membership is 80p a year but any other child in the same family pays 15p; out of London members 50p; overseas members 30p.

Young Vic is part of the National Theatre Company and it presents both classical and experimental plays with a young company. They have other activities especially aimed at the younger members of the club. Tickets cost about 40p.

THEATRE IN THE PARKS

GLC organises over 600 different shows in the parks during the summer. These events include plays, conjurors, puppets, punch and judy and open-air cinema. On Saturday afternoons active participation is the thing. **Battersea Park Concert Pavilion** has theatre shows twice a day throughout the school holidays.

In the **Court Theatre** at Battersea Park there is a great deal of activity throughout the summer. It's worth keeping your eyes open to see just what is going on. **Marble Hill** also presents amateur and professional companies.

Regent's Park Open Air Theatre, Tel: 486 2431, well-known for its performances of Shakespeare, is open in the summer in the most marvellous setting in the middle of the park. Cross your fingers and hope for a heat wave—or bring rugs, cushions, food, thermos flasks and sweaters.

MUSEUMS

Bethnal Green has a really good collection of toy theatres.

British Theatre Museum has manuscripts, the relics of many famous actors, Sarah Siddons' make-up table and many of the props from shows.

London Museum has a splendid collection of theatrical costumes, props, posters and programmes as well as other fascinating things.

Pollocks Toy Theatre is the place to go for amusing cut-out theatres, suitable plays and figures.

Toys

Most children today have many elaborate and expensive toys, so it is always fascinating to see how children two hundred years ago, or even before that, amused themselves. In the British Museum you can see toys which have been preserved from 1000 BC, but most of the museums have collections from the last two hundred years since it was not until the end of the 18th century that people began to really think about toys for children. At the same time new techniques of making things were discovered, so this was a very important time for toy making. The museums listed below are all well worth a visit, and there is a section which lists particularly good toy shops in London.

MUSEUMS

Bethnal Green Museum has one of the best toy collections in the country. There are early educational toys, rocking horses, dolls and dolls' houses, puppets, shadow theatres, 'penny' toys, zoetropes—everything you can think of.

British Museum has one or two very old toys from Ancient Egypt, Greece and Rome.

Cuming Museum has a few early toys and there is a selection of cheap toys bought at Bartholomew Fair in 1894.

Horniman Museum has a collection of toys from all parts of the world. There is an earthenware rattle from Egypt, and kites from the Far East.

London Museum has a very good collection of toys from the last three centuries, including 'penny' toys, and expensive dolls' houses. Some of the toys belonged to Queen Victoria and Queen Mary when they were children.

Pollocks Toy Museum used to be a miniature theatre which staged plays adapted from real London productions. Today there are many toy theatres on show, and you can buy everything you need to make one yourself. There are peep shows, optical toys, magic lanterns and early projectors and many of the famous 'penny plain and twopenny coloured' Victorian Toy Theatre Sheets. Benjamin Pollock, the founder of the museum, used to get his daughters to paint the twopenny ones. The small shop sells replicas of some of the toys, and gingerbread men for you to eat. There are special shows for children on Saturdays, and on Thursdays for school parties.

TOY SHOPS
Paul and Marjorie Abbatt, 29 Marylebone Lane, W1, Tel: 486 6978—educational toys, and an intelligent selection of other toys. The staff are experienced with children and will advise on the right toy for the age group.

Cherry's, 62 Sheen Road, Richmond, Surrey, Tel: 940 2454 sometimes has Victorian toys.

A. S. Clarke's Dolls' Hospital, 16 Dawes Road, SW6, Tel: 358 2081 has many toys for sale at large discounts. Mr Clarke mends broken toys.

John Dobbie, 79 High Street, Wimbledon, SW19, Tel: .946 7981; 32 Putney High Street, SW15, Tel: 788 1101 sells sturdy, well designed toys and books.

Educational Supply Company, 233 Shaftesbury Avenue, WC1, Tel: 405 8524 isn't as dull as it sounds. Very good value for money, and sells educational toys and games together with a magnificent series of plastic relief maps.

James Galt, 30 Great Marlborough Street, W1, Tel: 734 0829 sells sensible, well designed simple toys for up to 8 years.

Hamleys, 200 Regent Street, W1, Tel: 734 3161 is a very large and famous toy-shop which sells everything imaginable in the way of toys for all ages.

Heal's, 196 Tottenham Court Road, W1, Tel: 437 7605 has a marvellous display of well designed toys, especially at Christmas.

Jubilee, 10 Pierrepont Arcade, N1 has a few old toys.

Owl and the Pussycat, 11 Flask Walk, Hampstead, NW3, Tel: 435 5342 is a fascinating little shop with all kinds of well designed toys and books for all ages.

Pollocks Toy Shop, 1 Scala Street, W1, Tel: 636 3452 is part of the toy museum. The shop sells replicas of toys on show in the museum as well as modern toys. Toy theatres are a speciality.

Tridias Toy Shop, 44 Monmouth Street, WC1, Tel: 240 2369 sells modern toys, many of them made of wood.

Traction Engines

Although there is a great number of enthusiasts in the country there aren't many to be seen in London. The **Science Museum** is probably the best place to go.

The **National Traction Engine Club** is an enthusiastic body whose main aim is to preserve as many steam-powered traction engines as possible. They manage to organise rallies at various places all over the country and are the best people to contact for information.

Expo Steam, a great steam engine rally, is occasionally held at Battersea Park.

Transport

There are probably more clubs and societies devoted to the preservation and restoration of out-moded forms of travel in this country than there are anywhere else in the world.

Many of these societies have had remarkable success in either taking over and running light railways such as the Bluebell Line, or in persuading the Government to grant a new lease of life to those threatened with closure.

Probably, unless you are already only interested in one particular means of transport, the best club to join is the **British Young Travellers Society.** It organises tours, weekend outings and holidays, using as many unusual means of travel as possible. Although the club is based in Southampton it is hoped that other branches will spring up. If you want to know if there is one in your area, write to the Secretary.

AIRCRAFT

MUSEUMS
Imperial War Museum has a good collection of German and Japanese fighter planes as well as a Mosquito, a Heinkel and a Lancaster bomber. It also has a doodlebug from the Second World War (V1) and the rocket bombs (V2) which were Adolph Hitler's secret weapons.
Salisbury Hall, just outside London, holds the prototype of the Mosquito which was designed and built there.
Science Museum has gliders, the Gloster Meteor F3, the first ejector mechanism, the Cody biplane (1912) and a model of the Concorde among other replicas and models.

BICYCLES

Science Museum contains the Shuttleworth Collection consisting of an amazing number of bicycles from the penny-farthing onwards.

CARS

CLUB

Veteran Car Club of Great Britain welcomes junior members under the age of 17. Every member is issued with a badge and a copy of the quarterly gazette which is full of information about what is going on. The aim of this club is to preserve, maintain and to drive veteran cars on the road. (A veteran car is one manufactured before 31 December 1904.)

It also organises the **Transport Flea Market** twice a year where accessories like old motor horns are bought and sold.

MUSEUM

Science Museum has some marvellous cars in an absolutely impeccable condition. They usually permit one of the collection to be used on the annual run to Brighton. (See **Calendar.**)

VISITS

To visit **Ford Motor Company** of Dagenham see **Conducted Tours.**

CABS

London General Cab Company has a small but good collection of London cabs from 1907 onwards.

COACHES

MUSEUMS

Gunnersbury Park Museum has a collection of coaches including those owned by the Rothschild family.
Kenwood House has a small number of coaches.
Royal Mews has the collection of State coaches and carriages, as well as harness and livery.
Science Museum has enough in its collection to give you an idea of the history and development of horse-drawn vehicles.

COMMERCIAL VEHICLES

CLUBS

Historic Commercial Vehicles Club preserves and maintains commercial vehicles.
London Bus Preservation Society is organised for those who are particularly interested in the London bus.
Omnibus Society which maintains vehicles, is concerned with all forms of passenger transport on the roads.

MUSEUMS

British Transport Museum is a fantastically good one. By walking round you can get a really good idea of the history and development of public transport of all kinds. Among the many exhibits are early trams and buses, including Old Bill, the London bus which carried troops in the First World War.

London Museum has a fascinating collection of fire appliances. One wonders why it is that London didn't burn down.

EVENT
London-Brighton Commercial Vehicle Run takes place in May.

MILITARY TRANSPORT
Imperial War Museum has a good collection of vehicles used for military purposes.

MOTOR CYCLES
Vintage Motor Cycle Club is open to anyone genuinely interested in veteran or vintage motor cycles. A yearly run is organised but the start is at Tattenham Corner, and so it is not strictly a London event.

RAILWAYS

MUSEUMS
British Transport Museum has a marvellous exhibition of trains and rolling stock. Amongst other exhibits there is the 'Mallard', the fastest steam train ever, which reached 126 m.p.h., and Queen Victoria's railway carriage, an unbelievably plush affair.

Science Museum has models made by James Watt in 1765 for his experiments on steam, the famous 'Puffing Billy', the oldest locomotive in the world, built in 1813, George Stephenson's 1829 'Rocket', and many other exhibits right up to prototypes of diesel-electric locomotives.

CLUBS
If you want to know anything about the societies interested in the preservation and restoration of railways get in touch with the Chairman of the **Association of Railway Preservation Societies,** Captain Peter Manisty. You will find him very helpful and he will be able to tell you which society nearest to you is keen to have young supporters. The following clubs in or around London all welcome young enthusiasts and most of them have their own railway lines and engines:

Bluebell Preservation Society
Bulleid Pacific Preservation Society
Great Western Society
Kent and Sussex Association
Locomotive Club of Great Britain
Merchant Navy Locomotive Preservation Society
Quainton Railway Society Ltd.
Stour Valley Railway Preservation Society

VISITS
Visits to engine sheds and signalling boxes and the control rooms at

Euston can be arranged by writing to the Public Relations Officer at any of the main line termini.

Visits to the Post Office Underground Railway can be arranged. (See under **Conducted Tours**).

EQUIPMENT

British Rail Collectors' Corner National Carriers Depot, Cardington Steet, NW1, Tel: 387 9400 has all sorts of things for sale—guards' lamps, clocks, notice boards and so on. (Open Tuesday-Saturday 9.00-17.00. Open until 19.00 on Thursday.)

MAGAZINES

There is an enormous number of magazines to do with transport. Some of these are: 'Motor Sport'; 'Old Motor'; 'Railway Magazine'; 'Railway World'; 'Transport Magazine'; 'Veteran and Vintage Magazine'.

Travelling Around London

Inland Waterways Association runs tow-path walks and trips besides organising working parties to improve London's canals. Membership for juniors (under 18) is £1.05 a year. (For river and canal trips see **Boats**.)

Junior Jaunts offer complete days out for those from 5-15 for £3.50 a day. This includes absolutely everything. London children often choose a day in the country while visitors tend to go for sight-seeing and boat trips. In the winter there are visits to theatres and pantomimes. Pottery lessons have turned out to be a popular addition to the programme.

London Transport's 100 Bus is a 1930s ST—type bus, now reconditioned and in service. A circular tour round the West End takes 45 minutes and starts from Horse Guards Avenue hourly from 10.00—19.00. The fare, 5p, 10p or 15p depends on the distance. Adults, of course, pay double.

London Transport's Golden Rovers issued most days of the year, give you almost unlimited travel on Green Line coaches when you really feel you have had enough of London.

London Transport's Red Rovers are fabulous value for money. For 25p if you are under 14 and 50p if you are older, you get a day's unlimited travel on all red central bus routes, including Red Arrow and suburban flat fare buses. They are available every day and can be bought 7 days in advance at almost any underground station or from London Transport Enquiry Offices.

London Transport Tours are another bargain. The tour, which has a guide on board, covers more than 20 miles of London. One starts from Victoria Coach Station every hour on the hour from 10.00-21.00. It costs 30p (50p if you are over 14), and is worth every penny of it.

Off-beat Tours of London have become an institution. Small parties are conducted round London by knowledgeable and amusing guides at the cost of 15p (30p for adults). Each walk takes about 1½ hours and there are 40 different routes.

Useful Information

EMERGENCIES
Dial 999 from any phone box (no money needed) and ask for fire, police, ambulance or doctor. You will be asked who you are and where you are. Don't get into a panic about this. It only takes an extra minute and, in the long run, it actually speeds things up.

CHEMISTS (all-night)
Bliss Chemist, 54 Willesden Lane, NW6, Tel: 624 8000
Boots, Piccadilly Circus, W1, Tel: 930 4761

DENTIST (24 hour service)
St George's Hospital, Hyde Park Corner, SW1, Tel: 235 4343

DOCTOR (24 hour service)
Charing Cross Hospital, Agar Street, Strand, WC2, Tel: 836 7788
Middlesex Hospital, Mortimer Street, W1, Tel: 636 8333
St George's Hospital, Hyde Park Corner, SW1, Tel: 235 4343

EYE TROUBLE (24 hour service)
Moorfields Eye Hospital, City Road, WC1, Tel: 836 6611

FINDING THINGS
If you find something in the street give it to a policeman or take it to a police station. If it is not claimed within a month, then it is yours.

HELP NEEDED
These are places to go if you are in trouble yourself:
Help International, 10 South Wharf Road, W2, Tel: 402 5233 will tell you the best people to approach for your particular problem.
International Travellers' Aid Association, 2 Weymouth Street, W1, Tel: 636 9722 helps any travellers who are in a mess. They also have kiosks at Liverpool Street and Victoria stations.
Release, 50a Princedale Road, W11, Tel: 229 7753 really deal with drug offences but will give other help.
St Giles' Centre, Camberwell Church Street, SE5, Tel: 703 5841 help young people whatever their problems.

Young People's Consultation Service, The Tavistock Centre, Belsize Lane, NW3 , Tel: 435 7111 ext. 327 gives free help for those between the ages of 14-23 who have serious emotional problems.

HELPING OTHERS
The following organisations are some of those who welcome the help of young people. Your local Director of Social Services can probably suggest others.

Crisis Lend-a-Hand, 20 Cambridge Park, E11, Tel: 989 9044 helps people who have housing problems, or people who, because of their health and age or emotional stress cannot manage on their own.

International Voluntary Service, 91 High Street, Harlesden, NW10, Tel: 965 1446 is only for those over the age of 16. Work involved is with the underprivileged, the old and the young as well as the lonely. There are work camps in Britain and Europe as well as work for qualified young people in other countries.

Jewish Youth Voluntary Service, 33 Henriques Street, E1, Tel: 709 9044 takes on various sorts of service projects.

Salvation Army, 101 Queen Victoria Street, EC4, Tel: 236 5222 always has an enormous number of projects going.

Shelter, 86 Strand, WC2, Tel: 836 2051 is always interested if you want to take part in its fund-raising activities.

Social Work Advisory Service, 26 Bloomsbury Way, WC1 is the place to go if you are thinking of social work as a career.

Task Force, Clifford House, Edith Villas, W14, Tel: 603 0271; 98a Avenue Road, NW3, Tel: 722 0056 undertakes local community projects besides giving help and friendship to the old and lonely as well as the disabled. People over 15 are welcome.

Young Men's Christian Association, Community Services Department, 37 Bedford Square, WC1, Tel: 636 4111 does a great deal of varied work.

Young Volunteer Force, Abbey House, Victoria Street, SW1, Tel: 222 6722

INFORMATION
During the school holidays ring Tel: 246 8007 for ideas.
For sporting and entertainment information ring Tel: 246 8041

TOURIST INFORMATION
British Tourist Authority, 64 St James's Street, SW1, Tel: 629 9191 for tourist information and literature (some free).

City of London Information Centre, St Paul's Churchyard, EC4, Tel: 606 3030 for free advice and literature.

London Tourist Board Information Bureau, 4 Grosvenor Gardens, SW1, Tel: 730 0791 (telephone only between 8.00-20.00)

London Transport Enquiry Offices at Euston, King's Cross, Oxford Circus, Piccadilly Circus, St James's or Victoria underground stations for free maps and leaflets, or from 55 Broadway, SW1, Tel: 222 1234.

TRAVEL INFORMATION

British Rail Travel Centre, 12 Lower Regent Street, SW1 deals only with personal callers.

For **London Transport** (see under **TOURIST INFORMATION**).

FOR ALL OTHER INFORMATION

Ring the **Daily Telegraph Information Bureau,** Tel: 363 4242.

LOST

If you yourself are lost or you have lost the person you are with, go to the police. If you only want directions and there isn't a policeman in sight, ask any woman who has a couple of children with her.

LOST SOMETHING

On a bus: go to London Transport Property Office, 200 Baker Street, NW1. It will take a day or two to turn up there. If you know the number of the bus you can always make enquiries at the bus terminus.
On a train: go to the main line terminus and make enquiries there.
In a taxi: go to the Lost Property Office, Penton Street, N1.
Anywhere else: make enquiries at a police station.

Viewpoints

If you want to feel on top of the world and look out over the rooftops of London, there are several places where you can feel superior by looking down and watching the world at your feet.
Alexandra Palace was built in 1873 and since then it has been used as a concert hall for BBC television and is now used by the Open University. Its huge bulk dominates Muswell Hill and from the terraces you will have a fine view of North London and the Home Counties. It is particularly exciting at night, with a sweeping view of lit-up London.
Monument, a memorial built by Sir Christopher Wren to commemorate the Great Fire of London in 1666 is 202 feet high—the exact distance from the base of the Monument to the baker's shop in Pudding Lane where the fire started. The Monument is a hollow column of stone with a platform at the top from which there is a marvellous view of the City and river. There are 311 steps to climb up to the platform. Don't go up if you are afraid of heights or crumbly-looking walls and steps.
The Post Office Tower near Tottenham Court Road was opened to the public in 1966. Its total height is 620 feet, 200 feet more than any other London building. The highest observation platform is 499 feet from the ground. At the top of the tower there is an automatic answering machine which gives all these statistics and more.

Two lifts shoot you up to the observation platform at great speed, and there are binoculars and large photographic maps to help you identify what you see—the whole of the London Basin laid out before you, as well as four counties.

Above the observation platform there is a revolving restaurant, but it is very expensive. No one under fourteen is allowed in the Tower without an adult.

St Paul's Cathedral is splendid. The height from the pavement to the top of the cross on St Paul's is 365 feet. You can climb up to the dome and walk round it both on the outside and the inside. The outside gives you a marvellous view of the City of London, the Tower of London and the river. The inside is the famous Whispering Gallery, 420 feet round, where, if you whisper close to the wall on one side, someone else on the other side can hear you clearly. If you feel energetic you can climb right up to the Ball and Cross, where you will get an even better view. There are 727 steps to climb up to the Ball.

Shell Centre on the South Bank near Waterloo has a public viewing centre on the 25th floor, 317 feet high. From there the whole of London will be at your feet, and you will have a wonderful view of the buildings on the north bank of the Thames—the Houses of Parliament, Big Ben, and so on, as well as being able to look across the buildings on the South Bank. Many people think Shell Centre is extremely ugly.

Westminster Cathedral, near Victoria Station, is the seat of the Cardinal Archbishop of Westminster. Its tower is 284 feet high, and you can walk up to the top for nothing, or use the lift for 10p. When you come down the tower, spare a few minutes to look at the Stations of the Cross, which are rather unusual. The style of the building, which is Byzantine, is unlike anything else in London.

VIEWPOINTS IN PARKS

From **Whitestone Pond,** which is at the top of the hill on which Hampstead is situated, there is a marvellous view across the heath and to London beyond.

In South East London, **Bostall Heath** and **Lesnes Abbey Woods** are the places to view the Thames from the other direction. Just north of Lesnes Abbey the Plumstead Marshes stretch away towards the Thames. You can't actually see the Thames from here, but the passing ships look like children's toys being pulled along a distant road. **Shrewsbury Park** has a marvellous vista of dockland from the Pool of London right down to Erith; and south of Shrewsbury Park, **Eaglesfield,** which is 400 feet above sea level, has a fine view over Kent.

In South West London **Richmond Park** is the place to go for a good view. From the Terrace Gardens on Richmond Hill there is a superb view of the Thames. Turner's famous painting of this view can be seen at the Tate Gallery.

Heathrow Airport is not the place to view London—but from the roof garden terrace you can watch planes landing and taking off at an average rate of one every two minutes. It is exciting to see the newest aircraft coming in from all parts of the world. A running commentary tells you what is going on.

Walking

It isn't until you look properly at a map of London that you can see just how far you can walk without using the streets. Many of the parks are almost joined on to each other (Hyde Park and Kensington gardens are, for instance); others like Primrose Hill and Regent's Park are only separated by a road. It's worth seeing just how far you go without crossing more than a specified number of roads.

It is also possible to walk along the canals. Regent's Park Canal stretches a very long way and the towpath is clear most of the way.

The river too offers you a great opportunity for walking. There is always a lot to see and you will get splendid views of London the whole time.

If you are the sort of person who likes being taken around in a fairly informal way try these organisations:

Architectural and Historical Walks begin with a lecture and are followed by a walk. It takes about three and a half hours altogether. The parties are limited to twenty so you should book a place in advance.

Dickens' London, organised by a member of the Dickens Fellowship, is an enjoyable and informative stroll round London. Contact the British Travel Association for this.

London Unlimited offer really original walks—including ghost hunts.

Love London organise walks in the city—informative and interesting—which last about 1½ hours.

Off-beat Tours of London organise a good, interesting tour in an informal way. It's very cheap and you'll find yourself looking at London in a new light. The 1½ hour walks, with 40 different routes cost 15p (30p for adults) and are on Sunday afternoons only in winter but summer evening walks are also arranged.

Ramblers Association are the people to go to if you want to get out of London at weekends. They really are a good organisation and will let you know of any groups active in your neighbourhood. They protect the interests of country walkers by keeping footpaths and rights-of-way open. Other activities include London walks, outdoor holidays and holidays abroad.

EVENT

London-Brighton Walk starts at Westminster Bridge at 07.00 on the third or fourth Saturday in May.

Windmills

It might surprise you to know that there are a few surviving windmills in the London area. Most of them have lost their sails and have been converted for storage and other uses. Some are in private hands, but a few have been restored. The mills given here can be seen clearly from nearby paths or lanes, but the owner's permission must be sought before you cross private property.

Arkley Windmill near Barnet is a complete towermill.

Brixton Windmill in Blenheim Gardens was built in 1816. It stopped working by wind power in 1860. Then a gas engine was installed to supply power and it continued working up to 1934. Now it has sails and new machinery and is on view to the public.

Bromley-by-Bow's Tidemill stands in Three Mile Lane. Built in 1776, it has been derelict since the Second World War. Some time ago it still had its original grinding machinery which was wooden built and operated by water-power.

Merton Watermill is now the property of a firm of fabric printers.

Upminster Smock Mill, built in 1803, has been preserved so that you can see the mill's machinery. If you are seriously interested you can see it by writing to the Town Clerk of the London Borough of Havering.

The reference room inside the Borough of Havering's Library in Laurie Square, Romford has a model of this mill as it was when it was fully operational in the last century.

Wimbledon Mill which stands in the middle of Wimbledon Common is a well-known landmark. Although it is not open to the public since the lower part has been converted into a house you can, nevertheless, get a good look at it.

Science Museum has several scale models of windmills, all of which show you how they actually worked. There is also a large-scale model of the postmill at Sprowston in Norfolk as it looked in 1924. One side of this has been cut away so that you can get a good look at the machinery inside.

Youth Centres

These are places run by the Inner London Education Authority for people who are over the age of 14. They are easy to join, although you should get the permission of your head teacher if you are still at school. The best thing to do if you are considering becoming a member is to look in and wander around and talk to the Warden or whoever happens to be in charge that evening. Most of them are open from Monday-Friday from about 19.00-22.00.

These centres really are good. There is a lot to do, first-class equipment and expert professional help. The classes which range from Car Maintenance to Beauty Culture run for three terms. You are expected to follow a course for the whole of this period and naturally preference is given to those people who are pretty sure they can manage it.

What does it cost? Well, it all depends on age. If you are between 14-16 it can cost as little as 4p a week, that is 25p a term or 65p a year.

These Youth Centres have busy social programmes, sporting fixtures and tournaments, music and drama, and facilities for refreshments—usually a coffee bar.

If you do not know where there is a centre in your area, get in touch with your local Youth Officer.

These are a *few* of the activities carried on at some of the many Youth Centres that have sprung up in the last few years:

Cowley Recreational Institute offers car and scooter maintenance, chess, brass and bugle bands, trampoline, angling, judo, fencing and radio and television maintenance.

Earlsfield Youth Centre offers photography, health and beauty, billiards and snooker, guitar tuition and film-making.

Ensham Youth Centre offers korfball, go-karting (designing, building and racing), gymnastics, sub-aqua swimming and basketball.

Southfields Youth Centre offers archery, Duke of Edinburgh Award Scheme, pottery, woodwork, canoeing, cookery, needlework and drama.

It must be emphasised that these are only a few of the activities that go on, and only a few of the places where they can happen. Provided there is enough demand, you can even suggest new classes if your own particular interest isn't catered for.

Index and Addresses

All public places like museums, art galleries, parks and churches have how-to-get-there information. Associations, societies, institutes and clubs have addresses and telephone numbers so that you can get in touch with them. Page references are underneath the travel directions so that if, for instance, you only wish to visit one museum, you can see which things we have suggested you might like to look at.

Although all the details were correct when this book was published, opening and closing times do sometimes change, so if you want to be absolutely sure your journey won't be wasted, remember you can get up-to-date information from the British Tourist Board, Tel: 730 0791 from 8.00-20.00

Amateur Fencing Association, 83
Perham Road, W14, Tel: 385 7422
P. 54

Amateur Swimming Association,
Acorn House, Gray's Inn Road, WC1,
Tel: 278 6571
P. 103

Anglers' Co-operative Association, 53
New Oxford Street, W1, Tel: 240 1339
P. 55

Antique Bazaar, 6 Church Street, NW8,
Tel: 723 7566
P. 32, 43, 71, 74

Antique Supermarket, 3 Barrett Street,
W1, Tel: 486 1439
P. 71, 74

Apothecaries' Garden, Swan Walk,
SW3, Tel: 352 5646
Tube: Sloane Square
Bus: 11, 39, 137
P. 56

Architectural and Historical Walks,
International House, 35 Shaftesbury
Avenue, W1, Tel: 437 9167
P. 119

Arkeley Windmill, Barnet
Tube: High Barnet and bus 107
(Monday-Saturday,) 107A (Sunday)
P. 120

Arsenal Football Club, Avenall Road,
N5, Tel: 226 3312; Supporters' Club
Tel: 248 0481
P. 60

Artists' Place Society, 17 Duke's
Road, WC1, Tel: 387 0161
P. 50

Arts Exhibition Bureau, 17 Carlton
House Terrace, SW1, Tel: 930 6844
P. 25

Arts Study Centre, Mrs R. Urdang,
Hodford Hall, Hodford Road, NW11,
Tel: 455 6930
P. 22

**Association of Railway Preservation
Societies** 2 Cleaver Square, SE11, Tel:
735 5012
P. 113

Auto-Cycle Union, 31 Belgrave Square,
SW1, Tel: 235 7636
P. 76

Avery Hill, Bexley Road, SE9, Tel:
850 2666

Open: daily (winter) 11.00-16.30;
(spring) 11.00-18.30; (summer)
11.00-20.30
Closed: Christmas Day
British Rail: Falcon Wood (from
Charing Cross or Waterloo)
P. 56

Ballet Rambert, 96 Chiswick High
Road, W4, Tel: 995 4246
P. 50

Bank of England, Threadneedle Street,
EC2.
Tube: Bank
Bus: 6, 8, 9, 9A, 11, 15, 21, 22, 25,
43, 76, 133, 501, 502
P. 63-4

Banqueting Hall, Whitehall, SW1.
Open: Monday-Saturday 10.00-17.00;
Sunday 14.00-17.00
Closed: Christmas Eve, Christmas Day,
Boxing Day
Tube: Charing Cross, Strand, Trafalgar
Square
Bus: 3, 11, 12, 24, 29, 39, 53, 59, 76,
77, 77A, 77B, 77C, 88, 159, 168, 170
P. 64

Barn Elms Reservoir, SW15.
Open: apply for permit to Metro-
politan Water Board
Tube: Hammersmith
Bus: 9, 9A, 33, 72, 73
P. 19, 55

Battersea Dogs' Home, Battersea Park
Road, SW11.
Open: Monday-Friday 9.30-17.00;
Saturday, Sunday (claims only)
14.00-16.00
Tube: Sloane Square and bus 137;
Vauxhall and bus 44, 170
P. 19

Battersea Park, SW11.
Festival Gardens and Funfair
Open: Easter-Setember 12.00-late
evening
Children's Zoo, Tel: 228 9957
Open: Easter-September Monday-
Friday 12.00-18.00; Saturday, Sunday
12.00-19.00; Spring and Late Summer
Holiday Mondays 10.30-19.00

123

Concert Pavilion
Open: Summer months, Saturday,
Sunday 19.30; Sunday (July only)
15.00
P. 9, 10, 11, 17, 18, 19, 27, 28, 29, 48,
50, 55, 70, 78, 86, 95, 97, 108, 111
Battersea Sports Centre, Hope Street,
SW11, Tel: 228 8971
P. 54
Beaver House, Great Trinity Lane,
EC4, Tel: 236 3223
Tube: Mansion House
Bus: 6, 9, 11, 15, 18, 76, 513
P. 81
H.M.S. Belfast, Syon's Wharf, Vine
Lane (off Tooley Street), SE1.
Open: daily 11.00-18.00
Closed: Christmas Day
Tube: London Bridge
Bus: 42, 47, 70, 78
P. 30
Bermondsey Market, Bermondsey
Square, Tower Bridge Road, SE1.
Open: Friday 6.00-13.00
Tube: London Bridge
Bus: 1, 1A, 42, 78, 188, 188A
P. 71, 72
Berwick Market, Berwick Street, Soho,
W1.
Open: Monday-Saturday all day
Tube: Piccadilly Circus, Tottenham
Court Road
Bus: 14, 19, 22, 38
P. 73
Bethnal Green Museum, Cambridge
Heath Road, E2, Tel: 980 2415
Open: Monday-Saturday 10.00-18.00;
Sunday 14.30-18.00
Closed: Good Friday, Christmas Eve,
Christmas Day, Boxing Day
Tube: Bethnal Green
Bus: 8, 8A, 106, 253
P. 21, 22, 47, 51, 75, 80, 94, 108, 109
Billingsgate Market, Lower Thames
Street, EC3.
Tube: Monument
Bus: 8A, 10, 21, 35, 40, 40A, 43, 44,
47, 48, 95A, 133, 501, 513
P. 72, 99
Blackheath, SE3
British Rail: Blackheath (from Charing
Cross or Waterloo)

Bus: 53, 54, 75, 89, 108, 108B, 192
P. 9, 11, 12, 48, 62, 86
Bluebell Railway Preservation Society,
Mr J. Potter, 16 Gouett Avenue,
Shepperton, Middlesex.
P. 113
Bond Street Antique Centre, 124 New
Bond Street, W1, Tel: 629 1819
P. 71, 74
Borough Market, Borough High Street,
SE1.
Tube: London Bridge
Bus: 8A, 10, 18, 21, 35, 40, 40A, 43,
44, 47, 95A, 133, 501, 513
P. 57, 73
Bostall Heath and Woods, SE2
British Rail: Plumstead (from Charing
Cross, London Bridge or Waterloo) and
bus 99
P. 48, 89, 118
**British Association of Young
Scientists,** 20 Great Smith Street, SW1,
Tel: 799 7657.
P. 97
British Canoe Union, 26 Park Crescent,
W1, Tel: 580 4710.
P. 38-9
British Cycling Federation, 26 Park
Crescent, W1, Tel: 636 4602.
P. 49
British Drama League, 9 Fitzroy Square,
W1, Tel: 387 2666.
P. 107
British Field Archery Association, Mrs
D. Wilcox, Perscourt, Jenkins Lane, St
Leonards, Tring, Herts.
P.28
British Judo Association, 26 Park
Crescent, W1, Tel: 580 7585
P. 71
British Museum, Great Russell Street,
WC1, Tel: 636 1555.
Open: Monday-Saturday 10.00-17.00;
Sunday 14.30-18.00
Closed: Good Friday, Christmas Eve,
Christmas Day
Tube: Goodge Street, Holborn,
Russell Square, Tottenham Court Road
Bus: 68, 77, 77A, 77B, 77C, 170, 188,
196, 239 (to Southampton Row); 5, 7,
8, 19, 22, 25, 38, 55 (to New Oxford
Street)

P. 21, 32-3, 42, 44, 61, 71, 94, 101, 109

British Numismatic Society, 63 West Way, Edgware, Middlesex.
P. 44

British Piano and Musical Museum, 368 High Street, Brentford, Middlesex, Tel: 560 8108.
Open: March-November Thursday, Saturday, Sunday 14.30-18.00
Tube: Gunnersbury and bus 117, 267; South Ealing and bus 65
Bus: 116, E1, E2
P. 77

British Rail—for visits to engine sheds write to the Divisional Manager of the region concerned.
King's Cross Station, Divisional Manager, Great Northern House, 79-81 Euston Road, NW1, Tel: 837 4200.
Liverpool Street Station, Divisional Manager, 155 Bishopsgate, EC2, Tel: 247 7600.
(For other regions see Telephone Directory or British Rail Timetable.)
P. 45, 113-14

British Sub-Aqua Club, 160 Great Portland Street, W1, Tel: 636 5667.
P. 103-4

British Tenpin Bowling Association, 212 Lower Clapton Road, E5, Tel: 985 2115.
P. 104

British Theatre Museum, Leighton House, 12 Holland Park Road, Kensington, W14, Tel: 602 3052.
Open: Tuesday, Thursday, Saturday 11.00-17.00
Closed: Easter Saturday, Christmas Day, Boxing Day
Tube: Kensington High Street
Bus: 9, 27, 28, 31, 33, 49, 73, 207A
P. 47, 108

British Transport Museum, Clapham High Street, SW4, Tel: 622 3241.
Open: Monday-Saturday 10.00-17.30
Closed: Sunday, Good Friday, Christmas Day
Tube: Clapham Common, Clapham North
Bus: 35, 37, 45, 88, 118, 118A, 155, 189

P. 10, 93, 112-13

British Waterways Board, Delamere Terrace, W2, Tel: 286 6101
P. 29-30

British Young Travellers' Society, The Secretary, Mr D. M. Hill, 41 Forest Way, Dibden Purlieu, Southampton.
P. 111

Brixton Windmill, Blenheim Gardens, Brixton Hill, SW2.
Open: daily 9.00-dusk
Closed: Christmas Day
Tube: Brixton (and short walk up Brixton Hill)
Bus: 50, 57A, 59, 109, 133, 159
P. 120

Brockwell Park, SE24.
Brockwell Park Lido, Tel: 274 7991
Tube: Brixton and bus 2, 2A, 3, 172; Clapham Common and bus 37
Bus: 40, 40A, 68, 196
P. 18, 56

Bromley-by-Bow Tidemill,
Three Mile Lane, Bromley-by-Bow, E3.
Tube: Bromley-by-Bow
P. 120

Brompton Cemetery, Brompton Road, SW3.
Tube: Fulham Broadway, South Kensington
Bus: 11, 14, 22, 28, 39A, 45, 49, 91
P. 61

Broomfield Museum, Broomfield Park, Palmer's Green, N13, Tel: 882 1354.
Open: Easter-September Tuesday-Friday 10.00-20.00; Saturday, Sunday 10.00-18.00: October-Easter Tuesday-Sunday 10.00-17.00 (or park closing time)
Tube: Arnos Grove
Bus: 29, 244, 298
P. 79

Bruce Castle Museum, Lordship Lane, N17, Tel: 808 8772.
Open: daily (except Wednesday, Sunday) 10.00-12.30, 13.30-17.00
Closed: Bank Holidays and Saturdays preceding Bank Holiday Mondays
Tube: Seven Sisters, Wood Green and bus 243
P. 101

Buckingham Palace, St James's Park, SW1 (*see also* Queen's Gallery, Royal Mews).
Tube: St James's Park, Victoria, Green Park, Hyde Park Corner
Bus: 2, 2B, 9, 9A, 10, 11, 14, 16, 19, 22, 24, 25, 26, 29, 30, 36, 36A, 36B, 38, 39, 52, 73, 74, 74B, 137, 149, 181, 185, 500, 503, 506, 507
P. 6, 11, 13, 84
BUFORA, The Secretary, Miss Christine Henning, 99 Mayday Gardens, SE3.
P. 58
Bulleid Pacific Preservation Society, Mr R. T. Price, 64 Kempshott Road, Streatham, London, SW16.
P. 113
Bunhill Fields Burial Ground, City Road, EC1.
Tube: Old Street
Bus: 5, 43, 55, 76, 104, 141, 214, 243, 271
P. 53
Burlington Arcade, W1.
Tube: Green Park, Piccadilly Circus
Bus: 9, 14, 19, 22, 38, 506
P. 64
Burlington House, Piccadilly, W1, Tel: 734 9052.
Open: Summer Exhibition and others Monday-Saturday 10.00-18.00; Sunday 14.00-18.00
Closed: Christmas Day, Boxing Day, and between exhibitions
Tube: Green Park, Piccadilly Circus
Bus: 9, 9A, 14, 19, 22, 25, 38, 506
P. 8, 10, 26
Bushey Park, Teddington, Middlesex.
Tube: Richmond and bus 27, 270; Wimbledon and bus 131, 155
Bus: 72, 111, 211, 216, 264
P. 19, 55, 86
Butler Museum, Harrow School, Harrow-on-the-Hill, Middlesex, Tel: 422 1465.
Temporarily closed for reorganisation. Telephone for opening times.
Tube: Harrow-on-the-Hill
Bus: 136, 186, 258, 286
P. 79

Camden Arts Centre, Arkwright Road, Hampstead, NW3, Tel: 435 2643.
Open: Tuesday-Friday 11.00-20.00; Saturday 11.00-18.00; Sunday 14.00-18.00
Closed: Bank Holidays, Christmas Eve
Tube: Finchley Road
Bus: 2, 2B, 13, 26, 113
P. 22, 93
Camden Passage, Islington, N1.
Tube: Angel
Bus: 4A, 19, 19A, 30, 38, 43, 73, 104, 141A, 171, 171A, 172, 188A, 214, 277, 279
P. 27, 40, 73
Camping Club of Great Britain, 11 Lower Grosvenor Place, SW1, Tel: 828 9232.
P. 38
Canine Defence League, 10 Seymour Street, W1, Tel: 935 5511
P. 20
Canonbury Tower, Canonbury Place, N1.
Tube: Essex Road, Highbury
Bus: 4, 19, 30, 38, 43, 73, 104, 171, 271, 277, 279
P. 64
Carlyle's House, 24 Cheyne Row, Chelsea, SW3, Tel: 352 7087.
Open: Wednesday-Saturday 11.00-13.00, 14.00-18.00 (or dusk if earlier); Sunday 14.00-18.00
Closed: Good Friday, Easter Monday, Spring and Late Summer Holiday Mondays, throughout December
Tube: South Kensington; Sloane Square and bus 11, 19, 22
P. 53-4
Cartophilic Society, The Secretary, 208 Vicarage Farm Road, Heston, Middlesex.
P. 40
Cecil Sharp House, 2 Regent's Park Road, NW1, Tel: 485 2206.
Open: Monday-Saturday 9.30-17.30
Closed: Sunday, Bank Holidays, Saturday preceding Easter Monday
Tube: Camden Town and bus 74, 74B
Bus: 3, 53
P. 50, 58

Cenotaph, Whitehall, SW1 (*see* Houses of Parliament).
P. 13

Central Association of London and Provincial Angling Clubs 9 Kemble Road, Croydon, Surrey, Tel: 686 3199.
P. 55

Central Council of Physical Recreation, 176 Great Portland Street, W1, Tel: 580 9092.
P. 28, 48, 105

Chapel Market, Angel, N1.
Open: daily (early closing Thursday, Sunday)
Tube: Angel
Bus: 4, 19, 30, 38, 43, 73, 104, 171, 172, 214, 277, 279
P. 73

Charing Cross Pier, Victoria Embankment, SW1, Tel: 839 5320.
Tube: Charing Cross, Strand
Bus: 1, 1A, 6, 9, 9A, 11, 13, 15, 77, 77A, 77B, 77C, 176, 505
P. 29

Charlton Athletic F.C., The Valley, Floyd Road, SE7, Tel: 858 1495.
British Rail: Charlton (from Charing Cross, London Bridge or Waterloo)
Bus: 51A, 96, 161, 161A, 177, 180 180A
P. 60

Chelsea Antique Market, 253 King's Road, SW3, Tel: 352 1425.
P. 32, 44, 71, 74

Chelsea F.C., Stamford Bridge, Fulham Road, SW6, Tel: 385 5545.
Tube: Fulham Broadway
Bus: 11, 14, 22, 28, 91
P. 60

Chelsea Old Church, All Saints, Cheyne Walk, SW3.
Tube: Sloane Square and bus 11, 19, 22; South Kensington and bus 39A, 45, 49
Bus: 39
P. 33

Chelsea Pottery, 13 Radnor Walk, SW3, Tel: 352 1366.
P. 94

Chelsea Royal Hospital, Royal Hospital Road, SW3, Tel: 730 0161 Ex. 46.

Buildings and Museum:
Open: Monday-Saturday 10.00-12.00, 14.00-17.00; Sunday 14.00-16.30
Closed: Good Friday, Easter Sunday, Christmas Day
Tube: Sloane Square
Bus: 11, 39, 137
P. 10, 44, 58, 64

Chessington Zoo, Chessington, Surrey.
Tube: Ealing Broadway, then bus 65; Richmond, then bus 65, 71
British Rail: Chessington South
P. 18, 56

Children's Theatre Workshop, Sydney Webb Teacher's Training College, Bulstrode Place, W1.
P. 22, 106

Chislehurst Caves, Chislehurst, Kent.
British Rail: Chislehurst (from Charing Cross, Waterloo or London Bridge)
P. 61

Chiswick Park, W4.
Tube: Hammersmith and bus 290
Bus: E3
P. 48

City Information Centre, St Paul's Churchyard, EC4, Tel: 606 3030.
Open: Monday-Friday 9.30-17.00; Saturday 10.00-16.00 (Easter-September); 9.30-12.30 (October-Easter)
Closed: Bank Holidays, Sunday
Tube: Mansion House, St Paul's
Bus: 4, 6, 7, 8, 9, 9A, 11, 15, 18, 22, 25, 76, 141, 501, 502, 513
P. 116

Clapham Common, SW4, Tel: 673 5398.
Tube: Clapham Common, Clapham South
Bus: 37, 88, 118, 155, 181, 181A, 189
P. 12, 55, 96

Cleopatra's Needle, Victoria Embankment, WC2.
Tube: Charing Cross, Strand
Bus: 109, 155, 168, 172, 184
P. 81

Clink Street, Southwark, SE1.
Tube: London Bridge
Bus: 8A, 10, 18, 21, 35, 40, 40A, 43, 44, 47, 48, 70, 95, 133, 501, 513
P. 81

Clissold Park, N16.
Tube: Finsbury Park, Manor House
Bus: 73, 106, 141, 171
P. 18, 55
Club Row, Sclater Street, Bethnal
Green Road, E1.
Open: Sunday morning until 14.00
Tube: Liverpool Street
Bus: 5, 6, 8, 22, 35, 47, 48, 67, 78,
97, 149, 243A
P. 19, 73
Cockpit Theatre and Arts Workshop,
Gateforth Street, Marylebone, NW8,
Tel: 262 7907.
P. 12, 23, 41, 50, 58, 70, 78, 106
Columbia Road Market, Hackney, E2.
Open: Sunday morning
Tube: Old Street, Shoreditch
Bus: 6, 35, 55
P. 57, 73
Commonwealth Institute, Kensington
High Street, W8, Tel: 937 1852.
Open: Monday-Saturday 10.00-17.30;
Sunday 14.30-18.00
Cinema
Open: Monday-Friday 12.15, 13.15,
15.00, Saturday 14.45, 15.50, 16.40
Closed: Good Friday, Christmas Eve,
Christmas Day, Boxing Day
Tube: Kensington High Street
Bus: 9, 9A, 27, 28, 31, 33, 49, 73
P. 40, 50
Contemporary Dance Workshop 17
Duke Road, WC1, Tel: 387.0161.
P. 50
Costume Society, Mrs Ginsberg,
Department of Textiles, Victoria and
Albert Museum, Cromwell Road, SW7,
Tel: 589 6371.
P. 47
Council for British Archeology,
8 St Andrew's Place, Regent's Park,
NW1,
Tel: 486 1527.
P. 63
Courtauld Institute Galleries, Woburn
Square, WC1, Tel: 580 1015.
Open: Monday-Saturday 10.00-17.00;
Sunday 14.00-17.00
Closed: Good Friday, Easter Monday,
Christmas Eve, Christmas Day, Boxing
Day

Tube: Euston Square, Goodge Street
Russell Square
Bus: 68, 77, 77A, 77B, 77C, 170, 188,
196, 239 (to Woburn Place); 14, 24,
29, 73, 176 (to Gower Street or
Tottenham Court Road)
P. 25
Covent Garden Market, WC2.
Open: Monday-Saturday from 5.30
Tube: Covent Garden
Bus: 1, 6, 9, 9A, 13, 15, 77, 77A,
77B, 77C, 176, 505
P. 57, 72
Note: Covent Garden Market is moving
to Nine Elms in 1973.
Cowley Recreational Institute, Cowley
Primary School, Normandy Road,
SW9, Tel: 735 4536 (after 14.00).
P. 41, 54, 121
Craft Centre, 43 Earlham Street, WC2,
Tel: 240 3327.
Open: Monday-Friday 10.00-17.00;
Thursday 10.00-18.00
Closed: Saturday, Sunday, Bank
Holidays
Tube: Covent Garden
Bus: 1, 14, 19, 22, 24, 29, 38, 176
P. 25, 94
Craft Workshop, 49 Shelton Street,
WC2, Tel: 240 2745.
P. 23
Crafts Council Gallery, 12 Waterloo
Place, Lower Regent Street, SW1, Tel:
839 5263.
Open: Monday-Saturday 9.30-17.30
Closed: Sunday, Public Holidays
Tube: Piccadilly Circus, Trafalgar
Square
Bus: 3, 6, 9, 9A, 12, 13, 14, 15, 19,
19A, 22, 38, 39, 53, 59, 88, 159, 505,
506
P. 25
Crawford Antique Market, 43
Crawford Street, W1, Tel: 723 2333.
P. 71, 74
Crewe House, Curzon Street, Mayfair,
W1.
Tube: Green Park
Bus: 2, 2B, 9, 9A, 14, 16, 19, 22, 25,
26, 30, 36, 36A, 36B, 38, 73, 74, 74B,
137, 500, 506
P. 64

Crosby Hall, Cheyne Walk, SW3, Tel:
352 0483
Open: Monday-Friday 10.00-12.00,
14.00-17.00; Saturday, Sunday
14.15-17.00
Closed: Christmas Day
Tube: South Kensington and bus 17,
45, 49
Bus: 11, 19, 22, 39
P. 81
Crystal Palace F.C., Selhurst Park,
SE25, Tel: 653 2223.
British Rail: Selhurst Park (from
Victoria)
Bus: 50, 68, 75, 130A, 130B, 154,
157, 159, 166, 190, 194B
P. 60
**Crystal Palace Park and National
Sports Centre,** SE19, Tel: 778 7148.
Open: daily 8.00-dusk
Children's Zoo
Open: Easter-September Monday-
Friday 13.30-17.30 (termtime);
11.00-18.00 (weekends, Public
Holidays and school holidays)
Concert Bowl, Tel: 836 5464
Open: June-August Sunday 19.30
Tube: Brixton and bus 2B, 3
British Rail: Crystal Palace (from
Victoria)
Bus: 2B, 12, 12A, 108B, 122, 137,
154, 157, 227, 249
P. 8, 9, 10, 14, 17-18, 28, 39, 48, 49,
55, 60, 71, 76, 78, 86, 100-101, 103
Cuming Museum, Walworth Road,
SE17, Tel: 703 3324.
Open: Monday-Friday 10.00-17.30;
Thursday 10.00-19.00
Closed: Sunday, Public Holidays
Tube: Elephant and Castle
Bus: 12, 17, 35, 40, 40A, 45, 68, 171,
176, 184, 196
P. 61, 63, 99, 109
Curtain Theatre, Commercial Road,
E1, Tel: 247 6788
P. 41, 95, 107
The Cut, Waterloo Road, SE1
Tube: Waterloo
Bus: 1, 1A, 4A, 68, 70, 76, 176, 188,
188A, 196, 501, 502, 504
P. 73
Cutler Street Market, Hounsditch, EC3.

Tube: Aldgate, Aldgate East,
Liverpool Street
Bus: 5, 6, 8, 9A, 10, 15, 22, 23, 25,
35, 40, 42, 44, 47, 48, 78, 95, 97, 149,
243A, 253
P. 71, 73
Cutty Sark, Greenwich Pier, SE10, Tel:
828 3445
Open: Monday-Saturday 10.00-17.00;
Sunday 14.30-17.00 (to 18.00 in
summer); Easter Monday 11.00-17.00;
Spring and Late Summer Holiday
Mondays 11.00-18.00; Good Friday,
Boxing Day 14.30-17.00
Closed: Christmas Eve, Christmas Day
Tube: Surrey Docks and bus 1A, 70,
108B, 188
British Rail: Maze Hill
Bus: 53, 54, 75, 177, 180, 180A, 185
P. 30
Cutty Sark Society, Palmerston House,
Bishopsgate, EC2, Tel: 588 5241.
P. 30
Cyclists Touring Club, 13 Spring
Street, Paddington, W2, Tel: 723 8407.
P. 49

Daily Mail, Public Relations Officer
(for tours), Carmelite House, Victoria
Embankment, EC4, Tel: 353 6000.
Travel: *see* Daily Telegraph
P. 45
Daily Telegraph, 135 Fleet Street,
EC4, Tel: 353 4242
Tube: Blackfriars
Bus: 4, 6, 9, 11, 15, 17, 45, 63, 141,
168, 168A, 502, 513
P. 45
Dance Centre, 12 Floral Lane, WC2,
Tel: 836 6544.
P. 50
Dance Theatre Commune, The Studio,
52 Dorset Street, W1, Tel: 486 3697.
P. 50
Danson Park, Bexleyheath, Kent.
British Rail: Welling or Bexleyheath
(from Charing Cross, Waterloo or
London Bridge).
P. 49
Department of the Environment, 2
Marsham Street, SW1, Tel: 212 3341,

799 7533 ex. 398 (Mr Hart for fishing permits).
P. 55, 63

Dick Whittington's Stone, Highgate Hill, N6.
Tube: Archway
Bus: 210, 271
P. 81-2

Dickens' House, 48 Doughty Street, WC1, Tel: 405 2127.
Open: Monday-Saturday 10.00-17.00
Closed: Sunday, Public Holidays, Christmas week
Tube: Russell Square
Bus: 19, 38, 55, 172 (to Gray's Inn Road); 17, 18, 45, 46 (to Guildford Street)
P. 33, 54

H.M.S. Discovery, Victoria Embankment, WC2, Tel: 836 5138.
Open: daily 13.00-16.30 (organised parties with guide)
Closed: Christmas Day
Tube: Temple
Bus: 109, 155, 172, 184
P. 30

Doll Club of Great Britain, Mrs G. Greene, Grove House, Iffley Turn, Oxford.
P.52

Downing Street, Whitehall, SW1,
Tube: Charing Cross, Strand, Trafalgar Square
Bus: 3, 11, 12, 24, 29, 39, 53, 59, 76, 77, 77A, 77B, 77C, 88, 159, 168, 170
P. 64

Drury Lane Theatre, Drury Lane, WC2
Tube: Covent Garden, Holborn, Temple
Bus: 1, 1A, 4A, 6, 9, 9A, 11, 13, 15, 68, 77, 77A, 77B, 77C, 170, 171, 172, 176, 188, 196, 239, 502, 513
P. 8

Duke of Edinburgh's Award, 2 Old Queen Street, SW1, Tel: 930 7681.
P. 52

Dulwich College Picture Gallery, College Road, SE21, Tel: 693 5254.
Open: May-August Tuesday-Saturday 10.00-18.00; Sunday 14.00-18.00; September 1st-October 15th and March 16th-April 30th Tuesday-

Saturday 10.00-17.00 Sunday 14.00-17.00; October 16th-March 15th Tuesday-Saturday 10.00-16.00
Closed: Sundays in winter, Public Holidays, several days at Christmas
Tube: Brixton and bus 3 (to Thurlow Road)
British Rail: West Dulwich
Bus: 37 (to Dulwich Village); 12, 12A, 78, 176, 176A, 185 (to Dulwich Library)
P. 25

Dulwich Park, SE21, Tel: 693 5737.
Travel: *see* Dulwich College Picture Library
P. 18, 28, 48

Eaglesfield, SE18
British Rail: Lewisham or Blackheath (from Charing Cross, London Bridge, Waterloo) then bus 89
Green Line: 701, 702 (from Victoria or Westminster)
P. 89, 118

Earl's Court Exhibition Hall, Warwick Road, SW5, Tel: 385 1200.
Tube: Earl's Court, West Brompton
Bus: 30, 31, 74, 74B
P. 8, 11, 13, 14

Earlsfield Youth Centre, Tranmere Road, SW18, Tel: 946 9807
P. 41, 121

East Street Market, Walworth, SE17.
Tube: Elephant and Castle
Bus: 12, 17, 35, 40, 40A, 45, 68, 171, 171A, 176, 184, 196
P. 73

Educational Puppetry Association, 23A Southampton Place, WC1.
P. 95

Electra House, The Telephone Manager, Commerce Division, Victoria Embankment, WC2, Tel: 836 1222 ex 2663.
P. 45

Eltham Palace, Court Yard, Eltham, SE9, Tel: 850 3861.
Open: May-October Thursday, Sunday 11.00-19.00; November-April 11.00-16.00

Closed: Christmas Eve, Christmas Day
and occasionally when in use
British Rail: Eltham (Well Hall)
Bus: 21, 21A, 61, 89, 108, 124, 124A,
126, 132, 160, 160A, 161, 161A, 228
P. 85
Eltham Park, SE9.
British Rail: Eltham Park (from
Charing Cross, London Bridge or
Waterloo)
P. 48, 89
Embroiderers' Guild, 73 Wimpole
Street, W1, Tel: 935 3281.
Open: Monday-Friday 10.00-17.00
Closed: Saturday, Sunday, Public
Holidays
Tube: Bond Street, Oxford Circus
Bus: 159
P. 47, 80
English Folk Dance and Song Society
see Cecil Sharp House
Ensham Youth Centre, Franciscan
Road, Tooting, SW17, Tel: 672 2131
(after 19.00).
P. 54, 121
Epping Forest (stretches Chingford-
Epping) Essex.
Tube: Loughton, Theydon Bois,
Epping or Walthamstow Central, then
British Rail to Chingford
Bus: 20, 20A, 69, 102, 121, 145, 167,
167A, 179, 191, 205A, 217A, 235,
242, 250, 254, 262
P. 19, 87
Epping Forest Museum, Queen
Elizabeth's Hunting Lodge, Rangers
Road, Chingford, E4, Tel: 529 6681.
Open: Wednesday-Sunday
14.00-18.00
Closed: Good Friday, Christmas Day,
Boxing Day
Tube: Walthamstow Central, then
British Rail to Chingford.
British Rail: Chingford (from
Liverpool Street)
Bus: 38 (from Victoria or Piccadilly
Circus); 102 (from Golders Green)
P. 19, 79
Ernest Read Music Association, 143
King Henry's Road, NW3, Tel: 722
9644
P. 76

Evening Standard, Production
Secretary (for tours), 47 Shoe Lane,
EC4, Tel: 353 3000.
Tube: St Paul's
Bus: 4A, 8, 22, 25, 141, 501
P. 45
Everyman Cinema, Holly Bush Vale,
NW3, Tel: 435 1525
Tube: Hampstead
Bus: 24, 63, 187, 268
P. 40
Express Dairy Farm, College Farm,
Regent's Park Road, N3
P. 45

Faraday Building, Telephone Manager,
Queen Victoria Steet, EC4, Tel: 248
4174.
Open: Monday-Friday 14.00-16.00,
18.00-20.00; Saturday 18.00-20.00,
Closed: Sunday, Bank Holidays
Tube: Blackfriars, St Paul's
Bus: 4A, 6, 6A, 9, 11, 13, 15, 18, 141
(to St Paul's Cathedral)
P. 45-6
Farringdon Road Market, Clerkenwell,
EC1.
Open: Monday-Saturday 10.00-16.00
Tube: Farringdon
Bus: 5, 17, 45, 168A, 170, 221, 243,
259
P. 32, 73
Fat Boy, Cock Lane, EC4.
Tube: St Paul's
Bus: 8, 22, 25, 277, 279, 501
P. 82
Fenton House, Hampstead Grove,
NW3, Tel: 435 3471.
Open: Monday to Saturday (except
Tuesday) 11.00-17.00; Sunday
14.00-17.00
Closed: Tuesday, Good Friday,
Christmas Day
Tube: Hampstead
Bus: 210, 268
P. 77
Finchley Children's Music Group, 11
Southern Road, Fortis Green, N2, Tel:
883 3535.
P. 77

Finsbury Park, N4, Tel: 800 4743.
Tube: Finsbury Park
Bus: 29, 141, 171, 210, 221, 241,
253, 259, 279, 298, W2, W3, W7
P. 28, 48, 55
Flamstead House see National
Maritime Museum
P. 91, 97
Fleet Building, Chief Superintendent,
London Inland Telegraphs, LIT/AB, 40
Shoe Lane, EC4, Tel: 829 3750.
P. 46
Fortnum and Mason, 181 Piccadilly,
W1, Tel: 734 8040.
P. 42
Ford Motor Company, Kent Avenue,
Dagenham, Essex. (For conducted
tours write or telephone Mr B. Smith,
592 3000 ex 2527.)
P. 46
Forty Hall, Forty Hill, Enfield,
Middlesex, Tel: 363 8196.
Open: Tuesday-Friday, Easter
Monday, Spring and Late Summer
Holiday Mondays 10.00-20.00;
Saturday, Sunday 10.00-18.00;
October-March 10.00-17.00
Closed: Good Friday, Christmas Eve,
Christmas Day, Boxing Day
Tube: Turnpike Lane and bus 231
Bus: 135, 135A
P. 64
Fulham F.C. Craven Cottage,
Stevenage Road, SW6, Tel: 736 7035.
Tube: Putney Bridge
Bus: 30, 74, 220, 255
P. 60
Fulham Palace, Fulham, SW6, Tel: 736
5821.
Tube: Putney Bridge
Bus: 14, 22, 30, 74, 85, 85A, 93, 220,
255
P. 85

Geffrye Museum, Kingsland Road,
Shoreditch, E2, Tel: 739 8368.
Open: Tuesday-Saturday, Easter
Monday, Spring and Late Summer
Holiday Mondays 10.00-17.00; Sunday
14.00-17.00

Closed: Good Friday, Christmas Day,
Boxing Day
Tube: Liverpool Street and bus 22,
48, 97, 149
Bus: 67, 243, 243A
P. 23
Gemmological Association, St
Dunstan's House, Carey Lane, EC2,
Tel: 606 5025.
P. 71
Geological Museum, Exhibition Road,
SW7, Tel: 589 3444.
Open: Monday-Saturday 10.00-18.00;
Sunday 14.30-18.00
Closed: Good Friday, Christmas Day
Tube: South Kensington
Bus: 14, 30, 39A, 45, 49, 74, 74B
P. 71, 79
George Inn, Borough High Street, SE1.
Tube: London Bridge
Bus: 8A, 10, 18, 21, 35, 40, 40A, 43,
44, 47, 48, 70, 133, 501, 513
P. 64
Gipsy Moth IV, Greenwich Pier, SE10.
Open: Monday—Saturday
10.00-17.00; Sunday 14.30-17.00 (to
18.00 in summer); Easter Monday
11.00-17.00; Spring and Summer
Holiday Mondays 11.00—18.00; Good
Friday, Boxing Day 14.30-17.00
Closed: Christmas Eve, Christmas Day
Tube: Surrey Docks and bus 1A, 70,
108B, 188
British Rail: Maze Hill
Bus: 53, 54, 75, 177, 180, 180A, 185
P. 30
The Glasshouse, 27 Neal Street, WC2,
Tel: 836 9785
P. 23
Golders Hill Park, North End Road,
NW11.
Tube: Golders Green and bus 210,
268; Hampstead and bus 268
P. 18, 19, 56-7, 87
Goldsmith's Hall, Foster Lane,
Cheapside, EC2, Tel: 806 8971.
Open: by appointment only
Tube: St Paul's
Bus: 4, 8, 22, 25, 141, 501, 502, 513
P. 8, 71
Gordon Medical Museum, St Thomas's
Street, SE1, Tel: 407 7600.

132

Open: Monday-Friday 9.00-17.00 (by application to Dean of Medical School or Curator)
Closed: Saturday, Sunday, Public Holidays
Tube: London Bridge
Bus: 8A, 10, 18, 21, 35, 40, 40A, 43, 44, 47, 48, 70, 95, 133, 501, 513
P. 97
Gover Cricket School, 172 East Hill, SW18, Tel: 874 1796.
P. 48
Great Western Society, Mr. K. McCormack, 196 Norwood Road, Southall, Middlesex.
P. 113
Greater London Parks Department, 2A Charing Cross Road, WC2, Tel: 836 5464
P. 18, 48, 50, 59, 60, 83, 85-6, 91, 105, 108
Green Park, SW1.
Tube: Green Park
Bus: 2, 2B, 9, 9A, 14, 16, 19, 22, 25, 26, 30, 36, 36A, 36B, 38, 52, 73, 74, 74B, 137, 500, 506
P. 27, 40, 87
Greenwich Borough Museum, 232 Plumstead High Street, SE18, Tel: 854 1728.
Open: Monday, Thursday, Friday, Saturday 10.00-17.00; Tuesday 14.00-20.00
Closed: Sunday, Wednesday, Public Holidays
British Rail: Plumstead (from Charing Cross, Waterloo or London Bridge)
Bus: 96, 99, 122, 122A, 124, 177, 180, 180A, 229
P. 79
Greenwich Old Royal Observatory, Flamstead House *see* National Maritime Museum
P. 90
Greenwich Park, SE10.
Open: 7.00-20.00 (or dusk)
Travel: *see* National Maritime Museum
During summer months there is a Thames pleasure launch from Westminster or Tower Pier.
P. 29, 65
Group 64, Youth Theatre Workshop,

203 Upper Richmond Road, Putney, SW15, Tel: 228 8437 (evenings).
P. 58, 106
Guildhall Museum and Art Gallery, Bassishaw High Walk, Basinghall Street, EC2, Tel: 606 3030.
Open: Monday-Saturday 10.00-17.00
Closed: Sunday, Public Holidays
Tube: Bank, Mansion House, Moorgate
Bus: 6, 8, 9, 9A, 11, 15, 21, 22, 25, 43, 76, 133, 501, 502, 513
P. 8, 9, 10, 11, 12, 13, 25, 42, 65, 82, 99
Gunnersbury Park Museum, Acton, W3, Tel: 992 2247.
Open: April-September Monday-Friday 14.00-17.00; Saturday, Sunday 14.00-18.00; October-March 14.00-16.00 daily
Closed: Good Friday, Christmas Day, Boxing Day
Tube: Acton Town
Bus: 15, 91, E3
P. 51, 112

Hackney Stadium, Waterden Road, Stratford, E15.
Bus: 6, 30, 236, S3
P. 76
Hainault Forest
Tube: Hainault, then bus 62, 150, 247A
P. 97
Ham Common, near Richmond, Surrey.
Tube: Richmond and bus 65, 71.
P. 87
Ham House, near Richmond, Surrey.
Open: April-September Tuesday-Sunday, Easter Monday, Spring and Late Summer Holiday Mondays 14.00-18.00; October-March Tuesday-Sunday 12.00-16.00
Closed: Good Friday, Christmas Eve, Christmas Day, Boxing Day
Tube: Richmond and bus 65, 71
Bus:
P. 57, 80, 87

Hampstead Antique Emporium, 12
Heath Street, NW3, Tel: 794 3202.
P. 71, 74
Hampstead Heath, NW3.
Tube: Hampstead, Golders Green and
bus 210, 268
Bus: 24, 46, 63, 187, 210, 268
P. 9, 11, 12, 19, 27, 55, 87
Hampton Court Palace, Middlesex, Tel:
977 8441.
Park and Gardens
Open: daily until 21.00 (or dusk)
**State Apartments, Great Hall, Great
Kitchen and Cellars**
Open: May-September Monday-
Saturday 9.30-18.00; Sunday
11.00-18.00; October Monday-
Saturday 9.30-17.00, Sunday
14.00-17.00; November-February
Monday-Saturday 9.30-16.00; Sunday
14.00-16.00; March and April Monday-
Saturday 9.30-17.00; Sunday
14.00-17.00
Closed: Good Friday, Christmas Eve,
Christmas Day, Boxing Day
**Banqueting Hall and Tudor Tennis
Court**
Open: April-September (times as
above)
Maze
Open: daily 9.30—15 minutes before
closing of gardens
Bus: 72, 111, 131, 155, 201, 206,
211, 216, 264, 267
P. 29, 42, 55,57, 62, 85
Hayward Gallery, South Bank,
Waterloo, SE1, Tel: 928 3144.
Open: Monday-Saturday 10.00-18.00;
(except Tuesday and Thursday until
20.00); Sunday 12.00-18.00
Closed: Good Friday, Christmas Eve,
Christmas Day
Tube: Charing Cross, Waterloo
Bus: 1A, 4, 68, 70, 76, 149, 168A, 171,
176, 188, 196, 239, 501, 502, 503,
505, 507, 513
P. 25
Health Exhibition Centre, 90
Buckingham Palace Road, SW1, Tel:
730 5134.
Open: Monday-Friday 10.00-17.00
Closed: Saturday, Sunday, Bank

Holidays
Tube: Victoria
Bus: 2, 2B, 10, II, 16, 24,
25, 26, 29, 36, 36A, 36B, 38,
39, 52, 149, 181, 185, 500,
506, 507
P. 97
Heath Street, Hampstead, NW3 *see*
Hampstead Heath
Heathrow Airport, Middlesex.
Roof Garden
Open: daily 10.00-dusk (conducted
tours from 10.00-16.00 for parties)
Tube: Hounslow West and bus A 1
(express), 82
Green Line: 704, 705
P. 118
Henry VIII's Wine Cellar, Whitehall,
SW1.
Open: Easter-mid-December Saturday
14.30 (apply to the Secretary, Dept.
A.3/8 Department of the Environment,
Lambeth Bridge House, SE1)
Tube: Charing Cross, Strand, Trafalgar
Square, Westminster
Bus: 3, 11, 12, 24, 29, 39, 53, 56, 76,
77, 77A, 77B, 77C, 88, 159, 168, 170
P. 82
Herne Hill, Burbage Road, SE24
Tube: Brixton, then bus 37
Bus: 2, 2A, 3, 40, 40A, 68, 172, 196
to Herne Hill Station
P. 28, 49
Highbury Grove Youth Centre,
Highbury Grove School, Highbury
Grove, N5, Tel: 359 2915.
P. 70
Highgate Cemetery, Swains Lane,
N6.
Tube: Archway
Bus: 210, 271
P. 54, 62, 92
Hire Service Shops, Head Office, Essex
Road, W3, Tel: 992 0101.
(For other branches see telephone
directory.)
P. 38, 49
Historic Commercial Vehicles Club,
The President, Michael Banfield, 32
Acland Crescent, Denmark Hill, SE5,
Tel: 639 5261.
P. 112

Hogarth's House, Hogarth Lane,
Chiswick, W4, Tel: 994 6757.
Open: April-September Monday-
Saturday 11.00-18.00; Sunday
14.00-18.00; October-March Monday-
Saturday 11.00-17.00; Sunday
14.00-17.00
Closed: Good Friday, Christmas Eve,
Christmas Day, Boxing Day
Tube: Hammersmith and
bus 290
P. 54
Holborn Bars, High Holborn, WC1.
Tube: Holborn
Bus: 8, 22, 25, 68, 77, 77A
P. 65
Holland Park, W8.
Tube: Holland Park, Kensington High
Street
Bus: 9, 9A, 12, 27, 28, 31, 33, 49, 73, 88
P. 18, 27, 48, 50, 57, 78, 87-8
Hollow Ponds, Whipps Cross, E17.
Bus: 20, 20A, 48, 262
P. 55
Holy Sepulchre, Holborn Viaduct,
EC1.
Tube: Chancery Lane
Bus: 8, 22, 25, 501
P. 12, 13, 76, 82
Hornfair, SE7.
British Rail: Lewisham or Blackheath
(from Charing Cross, London Bridge or
Waterloo) and bus 89
Green Line: 701, 702 (from Victoria
or Westminster)
P. 89
Horniman Museum, 100 London Road,
Forest Hill, SE23, Tel: 699 2339
Open: Monday-Saturday 10.30-18.00;
Sunday 14.00-18.00
Closed: Christmas Eve, Christmas Day
British Rail: Forest Hill (from Charing
Cross, London Bridge, Waterloo)
Bus: 12, 12A, 63, 176, 176A, 185
P. 23, 47, 51, 56, 77, 79, 80, 109
Horse Guards, Whitehall, SW1 *see*
Henry VIII's Wine Cellar
P. 6, 11, 19
Horticultural Halls, Greycoat Street
and Vincent Square, SW1, Tel: 834
4333.
Tube: St James's Park, Victoria

Bus: 2, 2B, 10, 11, 24, 26, 29, 36,
36A, 36B, 39, 149 181, 185, 503, 507
P. 8, 10, 58, 102
Houses of Parliament, Parliament
Square, SW1.
When neither house is sitting
Open: Saturdays, Easter Monday and
Tuesday, Spring and Late Summer
Holiday Mondays, on Monday,
Tuesday, Thursday in August and on
Thursday in September 10.00-17.00.
Conducted tours Saturday and other
days if guides available.
During sessions
Open: admission to Strangers' Gallery
in either house by advance application
to an MP or a Peer or by queuing at St
Stephen's Entrance. Head of Queue for
Lords admitted from about 14.40 on
Monday-Wednesday and 15.10 on
Thursday. Head of queue for
Commons admitted Monday-Thursday
at about 16.15 and Friday from about
11.30.
Westminster Hall
During sessions
Open: Monday-Thursday 10.00-13.30,
Saturday 10.00-17.00
In recess
Open: Monday-Friday 10.00-16.00,
Saturday 10.00-17.00
Tube: Westminster
Bus: 3, 11, 12, 24, 29, 39, 53, 59, 76,
77, 77A, 77B, 77C, 88, 109, 155, 159,
170 172, 177, 184, 503
P. 13, 65, 66
Hyde Park, W2.
Lido (Serpentine)
Open: May-September daily 6.30-1 hour
hour before dusk
Tube: Marble Arch, Hyde Park
Corner, Lancaster Gate, Knightsbridge
Bus: 2, 2B, 6, 7, 8, 9, 9A, 12, 14, 15,
16, 19, 22, 25, 26, 30, 36, 36A, 36B,
38, 52, 73 74, 74B, 88, 137, 500, 616
P. 10, 11, 13, 21, 27, 55, 56, 88, 92

**Imperial College of Science and
Technology,** Prince Consort Road,
SW7, Tel: 589 5111.
Tube: South Kensington

135

Bus: 9, 9A, 52, 73
P. 10
Imperial War Museum, Lambeth Road,
SE1, Tel: 735 8922.
Open: Monday-Saturday 10.00-18.00;
Sunday 14.00-18.00
Closed: Good Friday, Christmas Eve,
Christmas Day, Boxing Day
Tube: Elephant and Castle, Lambeth
North
Bus: 3, 10, 44, 59, 109, 155, 172
P. 21, 40, 44, 75, 93, 111, 113
Industrial Health and Safety Centre, 97
Horseferry Road, SW1, Tel: 828 9255.
Open: Monday-Friday 10.00-16.30
Closed: Saturday, Sunday, Bank
Holidays
Tube: St James's Park
Bus: 11, 24, 29, 39, 503 (to Strutton
Ground); 10, 88, 149, 507 (to
Horseferry Road)
P. 97
Inland Waterways Association, 114
Regent's Park Road, NW1, Tel: 586
2510.
P. 114
Institute of Contemporary Art, Nash
House, The Mall, SW1, Tel: 839 5344.
Open: Tuesday-Saturday 12.00-20.00;
Sunday 14.00-22.30
Closed: Good Friday, Christmas Eve,
Christmas Day, Boxing Day
Tube: Piccadilly Circus, Trafalgar
Square
Bus: 1A, 3, 6, 9, 9A, 11, 12, 13, 15,
24, 29, 39, 53, 59, 77, 77A, 77B, 77C,
88, 159, 168, 170, 176, 505
P. 40
Institute of Domestic Arts, 160
Stewarts Road, SW8,
Tel: 720 1983
P. 80
Insurance Museum, 20 Aldermanbury,
EC2,
Tel: 606-3835
Open: Monday-Friday 09.15-17.15
Closed: Saturday, Sunday, Public
Holidays
Tube: Bank, Moorgate
Bus: 6, 8, 9, 9A, 11, 15, 21, 22, 25,
43, 76, 133, 501, 502, 515
P. 82

Inter-Action, 14 Talacre Road, NW5,
Tel: 267 1422.
P. 23, 69
Inverness Street Market, Inverness
Street, Camden Town, NW1.
Tube: Camden Town
Bus: 3, 24, 31, 53, 68, 74, 74B
P. 73
Islington Boat Club, 'The Water
Gypsy', City Road Basin, Regent's
Canal, N1. Enrolments: Mrs June
Webb, 22 Highbury Terrace, N5, Tel:
226 8962.
P. 30, 39
Iveagh Bequest, Kenwood House,
Hampstead Lane, NW3, Tel: 348 1286.
Open: April-September Monday-
Saturday 10.00-19.00 Sunday
14.00-17.00; October-March Monday-
Saturday 10.00-17.00 Sunday
14.00-17.00
Closed: Good Friday, Christmas Eve,
Christmas Day
Tube: Archway or Golders Green and
bus 210
P. 25-6, 78, 87, 112

Jason's Trip, 60 Blomfield Road, W9,
Tel: 286 3428.
Tube: Warwick Avenue
Bus: 6, 8, 16, 176, 187, 616
P. 29
Jenny Wren, 250 Camden High Street,
London, NW1, Tel: 485 6210.
Tube: Camden Town
Bus: 3, 24, 27, 29, 31, 53, 68, 74,
74B, 134, 137, 214, 253
P. 29
Jewel Tower, Old Palace Yard, SW1,
Tel: 839 2201.
Open: Monday-Saturday 10.30-16.00
Closed: Christmas Day, Boxing Day,
Sunday
Tube: Westminster
Bus: 3, 11, 12, 24, 29, 39, 53, 59, 76,
77, 77A, 77B, 77C, 88, 109, 155, 159,
168, 170, 172, 177, 184, 503
P. 65
Jewish Museum, Woburn House, Upper
Woburn Place, WC1, Tel: 387 3081.
Open: Monday-Thursday 14.30-17.00;

Friday and Sunday 10.30-12.45
Closed: Saturday, Jewish Holy Days,
Bank Holidays
Tube: Euston, Euston Square, Russell
Square
Bus: 14, 18, 30, 68, 73, 77, 77A, 77B,
77C, 170, 188, 196, 239
P. 65
Dr Johnson's House, 17 Gough Square,
EC4, Tel: 353 3745.
Open: May-September Monday-
Saturday 10.30-17.00; October-April
10.30-16.30
Closed: Sunday, Bank Holidays
Tube: Blackfriars
Bus: 4A, 6, 9, 9A, 11, 15, 502, 513
P. 54
Junior Jaunts, 13A Harriet Walk,
Sloane Street, SW1, Tel: 235 4750.
P. 114

Keats House, Keats Grove, Hampstead,
NW3, Tel: 435 2062.
Open: Monday-Saturday 10.00-18.00
Closed: Sunday, Good Friday, Easter
Saturday, Christmas Day, Boxing Day
Tube: Belsize Park, Hampstead
Bus: 24, 46, 187, 268
P. 33, 54
Kelvin House, Judd Street, WC1.
Public Relations Officer (for tours),
London Telephones, Camelford House,
87 Albert Embankment, SE1, Tel: 587
8000 ex. 7290.
Tube: King's Cross, Russell Square
Bus: 14, 30, 73, 77A, 77C, 239
P. 46
Kensington Antique Market, 49
Kensington High Street, W8, Tel: 937
5000.
P. 44, 71, 74
Kensington Gardens, W2 and W8.
Tube: High Street Kensington,
Lancaster Gate, Notting Hill Gate,
Queensway
Bus: 9, 9A, 12, 27, 28, 31, 33, 49, 52,
73, 88
P. 27, 88
Kent and Sussex Association, Mr. P.
Davis, 24 Hopgarden Road, Tonbridge,
Kent.
P. 113

Kenwood House, *see*
Iveagh Bequest
Kew Gardens, Palace and Queen's
Cottage, Kew, Surrey, Tel: 940 1171.
Gardens
Open: daily 10.00-20.00 (or dusk)
Closed: Christmas Day
Houses
Open: Monday-Saturday 10.00-16.50
(or dusk); Sunday 10.00-17.50 (or
dusk)
Closed: Good Friday, Christmas Eve,
Christmas Day, Boxing Day
Palace
Open: April-September, Saturday,
Sunday, Easter Monday, Spring and
Summer Late Holiday Mondays
14.00-18.00
Closed: October-March
Tube: Kew Gardens
Bus: 15, 27, 65, 90, 90B
River: river boat service from
Westminster Pier throughout the
summer.
P. 51, 57, 79, 85
Kew Green, Kew, Surrey
Travel: see Kew Gardens
P. 48
King George's Fields, Stepney, E3
Tube: Mile End
Bus: 5, 10, 15, 23, 25, 40, 40A, 86,
106, 277
P 28

Ladywell Centre, Ladywell Road,
SE13, Tel: 690 2887.
P. 28
Lambeth Palace, Lambeth Road, SE1,
Tel: 928 8282.
Open: occasionally—details in press.
Tube: Westminster and bus 3, 59A,
77, 77A, 77C, 159, 170
Bus: 10, 44, 149, 168A, 507
P.·85
Lamble Centre, Lamble Street, Kiln
Place, NW5, Tel: 485 7620.
P. 23
Lancaster House, Stable Yard, St
James's Palace, SW1.
Open: Easter-mid-December,
Saturday, Sunday, Easter Monday,

Spring and Late Summer Bank Holiday
Mondays 14.00-18.00
Tube: Green Park
Bus: 9, 9A, 14, 19, 22, 25, 38
P. 82
Law Courts, Strand, WC2, Tel: 405
7641.
Open: public galleries usually open
during legal terms Monday—Friday
10.30-13.00; 14.00-16.00
Tube: Temple
Bus: 1, 4, 6, 9, 9A, 11, 13, 15, 68, 77,
77A, 170, 171, 172, 176, 188, 196,
239, 502, 505, 513
P. 12, 13
Lawn Tennis Association, Queen's
Club, Baron's Court, W14, Tel: 385
2366.
P. 65, 105
Leadenhall Market, Gracechurch
Street, EC3.
Tube: Bank, Monument
Bus: 8A, 10, 15, 25, 35, 40, 47, 48
P. 72
Leaside Youth Centre, Springfield
Lane, Clapton, E5, Tel: 806 6887.
P. 39
Leather Lane Market, Leather Lane,
EC1.
Tube: Chancery Lane
Bus: 5, 8, 17, 18, 22, 25, 45, 46, 55,
171, 243, 259, 501
P. 73
Leathercraft Museum, Gillett House,
55 Basinghall Street, EC2, Tel: 606
3030.
Open: Monday-Saturday 10.00-17.00
Closed: Sunday, Bank Holidays
Tube: Bank, Mansion House, Moorgate
Bus: 6, 8, 9, 9A, 11, 15, 21, 22, 25,
43, 76, 133, 501, 502, 513
P. 48
Leighton House Art Gallery, 12
Holland Park Road, W14, Tel: 602
3316.
Open: Monday-Saturday 11.00-17.00
Closed: Sunday, Bank Holidays
Tube: High Street Kensington
Bus: 9, 9A, 27, 28, 33, 49, 73
P. 26
Lesnes Abbey Woods, SE2.
British Rail: Abbey Wood (from

Charing Cross, London Bridge,
Waterloo).
P. 89, 118
Leyton Orient F.C., Brisbane Road,
E10, Tel: 539 6800.
Tube: Leyton
Bus: 34, 58, 69, 236, 241, 278
P. 60
Liberty and Co. Ltd, Regent Street,
W1, Tel: 734 1234.
P. 42
Lincoln's Inn, Chancery Lane, WC2.
(Call at Porter's lodge before entering.)
Halls, Library and Chapel
Open: Monday-Friday 10.00-16.30
Closed: Saturday, Sunday, Bank
Holidays
Gardens
Open: Monday-Friday 12.00-14.30
Closed: Saturday, Sunday, Bank
Holidays
Tube: Chancery Lane
Bus: 8, 22, 25, 171, 501
P. 65, 92
Little Angel Marionette Theatre, 14
Dagmar Passage, Cross Street,
Islington, N1, Tel: 226 1787.
P. 95
Little Venice (Regent's Canal),
Paddington, W2.
Tube: Warwick Avenue
Bus: 6, 8, 16, 18, 187, 616
P. 10, 29
Locomotive Club of Great Britain, The
Secretary, M. Burton, 85 Balmoral
Road, Gillingham, Kent.
P. 113
**London Adventure Playground
Association,** 57B Catherine Place, SW1,
Tel: 834 0656.
P. 15
London Anglers' Association, 32
Stroud Green Road, Finsbury Park,
N4, Tel: 263 0196.
P. 55
London Bus Preservation Society, c/o
17 Air Street, W1, Tel: 437 8225.
P. 112
London Cigarette Card Company, 34
Wellesley Road, W4,
Tel: 994 2346.
P. 40

London Dolphinarium, 65 Oxford
Street, W1.
Open: daily 11.00-21.30
Closed: Christmas Day
Tube: Oxford Circus, Tottenham
Court Road
Bus: 1, 7, 8, 25, 73
P. 19, 56
London Football Association, 51
Barking Road, E16, Tel: 476 1750.
P. 60
London General Cab Co., 1 Brixton
Road, SW9, Tel: 735 7777.
Open: Monday-Friday 7.30-18.00
Closed: Saturday, Sunday, Public
Holidays
Tube: Oval
Bus: 3, 36, 36A, 36B, 59, 59A, 95,
109, 133, 155, 159, 172, 185
P. 112
London Jazz Association, The
Secretary, 10 Penton Road, Staines,
Middlesex,
Tel: Staines 53139.
P. 70
London Museum, Kensington Palace,
The Broad Walk, Kensington Gardens,
W8, Tel: 937 9816.
Open: March-September Monday-
Saturday 10.00-18.00 Sunday
14.00-18.00; October and February
Monday-Saturday 10.00-17.00
Sunday 14.00-17.00; November-
January Monday-Saturday
10.00-16.00 Sunday 14.00-16.00
Closed: Good Friday, Christmas Eve,
Christmas Day, Boxing Day
Tube: High Street Kensington,
Queensway
Bus: 9, 9A, 12, 27, 28, 31, 33, 49, 52,
73, 88
P. 21, 33, 34, 42, 48, 51, 62, 85, 93,
94, 108, 109, 113
London Natural History Society, The
Secretary, 40 Frinton Road, Kirby
Cross, Frinton-on-Sea, Essex.
P. 78-9
London Orchestral Association, 13-14
Archer Street, W1, Tel: 437 1588.
P. 77
London Planetarium, Marylebone
Road, NW1, Tel: 486 1121.

Open: April-September daily
11.00-18.00; October-March Monday-
Friday 11.00-17.00 Saturday, Sunday,
Good Friday, Boxing Day 11.00-18.00
Christmas Eve 11.00-16.00
(presentations every hour on the hour.)
Closed: Christmas Day
Tube: Baker Street
Bus: 1, 2, 2B, 13, 18, 26, 27, 30, 59,
74, 74B, 113, 159, 176
P. 46, 90
**London School of Contemporary
Dance,** 17 Duke's Road, WC1, Tel: 387
0161.
P. 50
London School of Flying, Elstree
Aerodrome, Boreham Wood,
Hertfordshire, Tel: 935 4411.
P. 58
London Silver Vaults, Chancery House,
Chancery Lane, WC2, Tel: 242 3844.
Open: Monday-Friday 9.00-17.30;
Saturday 9.00-12.30
Closed: Sunday, Bank Holidays
Tube: Chancery Lane
Bus: 8, 22, 25, 171, 501
P. 71
London Stone, Bank of China, Cannon
Street, EC4.
Tube: Cannon Street, Monument
Bus: 9A, 18, 95, 149, 176A, 513
P. 82
London Symphony Orchestra Club, 1
Montague Street, WC1, Tel: 636 1704.
P. 77
London Transport, 55 Broadway,
Westminster SW1, Tel: 222 1234.
Lost Property Office, 200 Baker
Street, NW1.
Open: Monday-Friday 10.00-18.00
Closed: Saturday, Sunday, Public
Holidays
Tube: Baker Street
Bus: 1, 2, 2B, 13, 18, 26, 27, 30, 59,
74, 74B, 113, 159, 176
Enquiries
Open: as above: night or day or at
    enquiry offices at King's Cross,
    Oxford Circus, Piccadilly Circus, St
    James's Park, Victoria Underground
    Stations.
Publicity Poster Shop, Griffith House,

280 Old Marylebone Road, NW1,
Tel: 262 3444.
Open: Monday-Thursday 9.00-16.30;
Friday 9.00-16.00
Closed: Saturday, Sunday, Public
Holidays
Tube: Edgware Road
Bus: 6, 7, 8, 15, 16, 18, 27, 36, 36A,
36B, 176, 616
Tours, Victoria Coach Station,
Buckingham Palace Road, SW1.
Tube: Victoria
Bus: 11, 39
P. 114-15
London Unlimited, 15 Hollybark Hill,
London Road, Sittingbourne, Kent,
Sittingbourne (0795) 71616.
P. 61, 119
London Wall,
All Hallows-on-the-Wall Church,
London Wall, EC2.
Tube: Liverpool Street
Bus: 11, 133, 502
Roman Wall House, 1 Crutched Friars,
EC3.
Open: Monday-Friday 9.00-17.00
Closed: Saturday, Sunday, Good
Friday, Christmas Day, Boxing Day
Tube: Aldgate, Tower Hill
Bus: 10, 15, 25, 40, 40A, 42, 78, 253
St Alphege Churchyard, London Wall,
EC2
Tube: Moorgate
Bus: 9, 11, 21, 43, 76, 133, 141, 502
P. 65
London Zoo, Regent's Park, NW1, Tel:
722 3544.
Open: March-September Monday-
Saturday 9.00-18.00; Sunday, Easter
Monday, Spring and Summer Late
Summer Holiday Mondays 9.00-19.00;
November-February 10.00-17.00 (or
dusk)
Closed: Christmas Day
Children's Zoo
Open: March-October Monday-
Saturday 10.30-17.30; Sunday, Easter
Monday, Spring and Late Summer
Holiday Mondays 10.30-18.15;
November-February Monday-Saturday
10.30-16.00; Sunday and Boxing Day
10.30-15.30

Tube: Baker Street, Camden Town
and bus 74, 74B
Bus: 3, 53
Canal: Zoo Waterbus, 'Jason' and
'Jenny Wren' (*see* under **Boats.**)
P. 16-17, 29-30, 56
Lord's Cricket Ground, St John's
Wood, NW1, Tel: 289 1616.
Tube: St John's Wood
Bus: 2, 2B, 13, 26, 59, 74, 74B, 113,
159, 187
P. 48
Love London, 2 Ashburn Gardens,
SW7, Tel: 387 9876
P. 119

Mansion House, Mansion House Street,
EC4, Tel: 626 2500.
Open: admission on certain Saturdays
by written application to the Lord
Mayor
Tube: Bank
Bus: 8, 9, 9A, 11, 15, 21, 25, 43, 76,
133, 501, 502
P. 11, 14, 65-6
Marble Arch, W1.
Tube: Marble Arch
Bus: 2, 2B, 6, 7, 8, 12, 15, 16, 26, 30,
36, 36A, 36B, 73, 74, 74B, 88, 137,
500, 505, 616
P. 62, 66
Marble Hill House and Park, Richmond
Road, Twickenham, Middlesex.
Open: Tuesday-Saturday, Easter
Monday, Spring and Late Summer
Holiday Mondays, Boxing Day
10.00-17.00; Sunday 14.00-17.00
Closed: Monday, Good Friday,
Christmas Eve, Christmas Day
Tube: Richmond and bus 27, 33, 73,
90, 90B, 202, 203, 270
P. 50, 108
Marlborough House, Marlborough
Road, Pall Mall, SW1, Tel: 930 9249.
Open: Easter-September Saturday,
Sunday, Easter Monday, Spring and
Late Summer Holiday Mondays
14.00-18.00 (Visits to house and
chapel arranged by application to the
Administration Officer.)
Tube: Green Park

Bus: 9, 9A, 14, 19, 22, 25, 38, 506
P. 66
Martinware Pottery Collection, Public
Library, Osterley Park Road, Southall,
Middlesex, Tel: 574 3412.
Open: Monday-Friday 9.00-20.00;
Saturday 9.00-17.00
Closed: Sunday, Bank Holidays
Tube: Osterley
Bus: 91, 110, 111, 116, 120
P. 94
Maryon Park and Maryon-Wilson Park,
SE7.
British Rail: Charlton (from Charing
Cross, London Bridge, Waterloo) and
bus 163, 177, 177A, 180
P. 18, 89
Matchbox Label Society, J. H. Luker,
283 Worpleston Road, Guildford,
Surrey.
P. 75
**Merchant Navy Locomotive
Preservation Society,** The Secretary,
Tony Clare, 331 Uxbridge Road, W3.
P. 113
Merton Watermill, Merton Fabric
Printers, Littlers Close, Merton, SW19.
Tube: Colliers Wood
P. 120
Metropolitan Water Board, New River
Head, Roseberry Avenue, EC1, Tel:
837 3300.
Open: Monday-Friday 9.00-16.00
(for fishing permits)
P.55
Miss Meyer-Michael, 30 Heathcroft,
Hampstead Way, NW11, Tel: 455
0817.
P. 94
Millwall F.C., The Den, New Cross,
SE14,
Tel: 639 3143.
Tube: New Cross Gate
Bus: 21, 36A, 36B, 53, 141, 171, 177,
180A, P1
P. 60
Minerva Youth Theatre, 21 Lindale,
Wimbledon Park Road, SW19.
Note: this address is for
correspondence. The group meets at
the moment on Monday and Friday at
Christopher Wren School; on

Wednesday at the Harrow Club.
P. 107
Moberley Youth Centre, Kilburn Lane,
W10, Tel: 969 4083.
P. 70
Monument, Fish Street Hill, EC3.
Open: April-September Monday-
Saturday 9.00-17.40 Sunday
14.00-17.40; October-March Monday-
Saturday 9.00-15.40
Closed: Good Friday, Christmas Day,
Boxing Day
Tube: Monument
Bus: 8A, 9A, 10, 21, 35, 40, 40A, 43,
44, 47, 48, 133, 501, 513
P. 66, 117
Moonrock, Free School, 164 Regent's
Park Road, NW3, Tel: 586 2715.
P. 23, 94, 106
Mount Pleasant Sorting Office, EC1,
Tel: 837 4272
P. 46
Mountview Theatre Club, 104 Crouch
Hill, N8, Tel: 340 5885.
P. 107

National Army Museum, Royal
Hospital Road, Chelsea, SW3, Tel: 730
2477.
Open: Monday-Saturday 10.00-17.30;
Sunday, Easter Monday, Spring and
Late Summer Holiday Mondays
14.00-17.30
Closed: Good Friday, Christmas Day,
Boxing Day
Tube: Sloane Square
Bus: 11, 39, 137
P. 21, 44
National Book League, 7 Albemarle
Street, W1, Tel: 493 9001.
Open: Monday-Friday 9.30-21.00
(during exhibitions 10.00-18.00)
Closed: Saturday, Sunday, Bank Holidays
Tube: Green Park
Bus: 9, 14, 19, 22, 25, 38, 506
P. 34
National Cricket Association, Lord's
Cricket Ground, St John's Wood Road,
NW8.
P. 48

National Film Theatre, South Bank, Waterloo, SE1, Tel: 928 3232.
Tube: Charing Cross, Waterloo
Bus: 1, 1A, 4, 68, 70, 76, 149, 168A, 171, 176, 188, 196, 239, 501, 502, 503, 505, 507, 513
P. 40

National Gallery, Trafalgar Square, WC2, Tel: 930 7618
Open: Monday-Saturday 10.00-18.00; Sunday and Boxing Day 14.00-18.00; June-September Tuesday and Thursday 10.00-21.00
Closed: Christmas Eve, Christmas Day
Tube: Strand, Trafalgar Square
Bus: 1, 1A, 3, 6, 9, 9A, 11, 12, 13, 15, 24, 29, 39, 53, 59, 77, 77A, 77B, 77C, 88, 159, 168, 170, 176, 505
P. 26

National Maritime Museum and Flamstead House, Romney Road, Greenwich, SE10, Tel: 858 4422.
Open: Monday-Saturday 10.00-18.00; Sunday 14.30-18.00
Closed: Good Friday Christmas Eve, Christmas Day, Boxing Day
Tube: Surrey Docks and bus 1A, 70, 108B, 188
Bus: 53, 54, 75, 177, 180, 180A, 185
British Rail: Maze Hill
P. 30-1, 42, 43, 44, 75, 90-1, 97
Note: During the summer months there is a Thames pleasure boat from Westminster and Tower piers.

National Philatelic Society, 44 Fleet Street, EC4, Tel: 353 7210
P. 102-3

National Portrait Gallery, St Martin's Place, Trafalgar Square, WC2, Tel: 930 8511.
Open: Monday-Friday 10.00-17.00; Saturday 10.00-18.00; Sunday 14.00-18.00
Closed: Good Friday, Christmas Eve, Christmas Day
Travel: *see* National Gallery
P. 53

National Postal Museum, King Edward Street, EC1, Tel: 432 3851.
Open: Monday-Friday 10.00-16.30; Saturday 10.00-16.00 (for tours apply to the Curator)

Closed: Sunday, Bank Holidays
Tube: St Paul's
Bus: 4, 8, 22, 25, 141, 501, 502
P. 46, 101

National Traction Engine Club, The Secretary, 127 Greensted Road, Loughton, Essex.
P. 110-11

National Youth Theatre, 81 Ecclestone Square, SW1, Tel: 834 1085.
P. 107-8

Natural History Museum, Cromwell Road, South Kensington, SW7, Tel: 589 6323
Open: Monday-Saturday 10.00-18.00; Sunday 14.30-18.00
Closed: Good Friday, Christmas Eve, Christmas Day, Boxing Day.
Tube: South Kensington
Bus: 14, 30, 39A, 45, 49, 74, 74B
P. 19-20, 71, 79

New Arts Lab, 1 Robert Street, NW1, Tel: 387 8980.
P. 70

News of the World, Public Relations Officer (for tours) 30 Bouverie Street, EC4, Tel: 353 3030.
Tube: Blackfriars
Bus: 4, 6, 9, 11, 15, 17, 45, 63, 141, 168, 168A, 502, 513
P. 46, 83

Oasis Swimming Pool, Endell Street, WC2, Tel: 836 9555.
Tube: Covent Garden, Tottenham Court Road
Bus: 1, 14, 24; 29, 73, 176 (south-bound); 7, 8, 19, 22, 25, 38 (westbound)
P. 103

Off-beat Tours of London, 66 St. Michael's Street, W2, Tel: 262 9572.
P. 115, 119

Old Bailey, EC4
Open: Public admitted when courts are sitting
Tube: St. Paul's
Bus: 4, 6, 7, 8, 9, 9A, 11, 15, 18, 22, 25, 141, 501, 502, 513.
P. 66, 99

Old Battersea House, Vicarage
Crescent, SW11.
Tube: South Kensington and bus 39A,
45, 49
Bus: 19, 39, 249
P. 94

Old Curiosity Shop, Portsmouth
Street, Kingsway, WC2, Tel: 405 9891.
Open: daily 9.30-17.30
Closed: Christmas Day
Tube: Holborn
Bus: 68, 77, 77A, 77B, 77C, 170, 172,
188, 196, 239
P. 66

Old Palace Yard *see* Houses of Parliament.

Olympia, Hammersmith Road, W14,
Tel: 603 3344.
Tube: Kensington (Olympia)
Bus: 9, 9A, 27, 28, 33, 49, 73 91
P. 8, 12, 13, 14, 38, 102

The Omnibus Society, R. J. Durrant,
78 Nightingale Road, Petts Wood,
Orpington, Kent.
P. 112

Operating Theatre (Old St. Thomas'
Hospital), Southwark Cathedral,
Chapter House, St. Thomas' Street,
SE1.
Open: Monday, Wednesday, Friday
12.30-16.00
Closed: Bank Holidays
Tube: London Bridge
Bus: 8A, 10, 18, 21, 35, 40, 40A, 44,
47, 48, 70, 133, 501, 513
P. 62, 98

Osterley Park, Osterley, Middlesex.
Open: daily 10.00-dusk
Tube: Osterley
Bus: 91, 116
P. 55, 66

Oval Cricket Ground, Kennington,
SE11, Tel: 735 2424.
Tube: Oval
Bus: 3, 36, 36A, 36B, 59, 95, 109,
133, 155, 159, 172, 185
P. 48

Oval House, Kennington Oval, SE11,
Tel: 735 2786.
Travel: *see* Oval Cricket Ground
P. 41, 50, 59, 70, 106

Paddington Recreation Ground, W9
Tube: Maida Vale
Bus: 8, 16, 176, 616
P. 49

Parliament Hill, NW5
Tube: Camden Town and bus 214
P. 9, 13, 28, 50, 87, 100, 101

Parliament Square, SW1.
Travel: *see* Houses of Parliament
P. 10

Passmore Edwards Museum, Romford
Road, E15, Tel: 534 4545.
Open: Monday, Tuesday, Wednesday,
Friday 10.00-18.00; Thursday
10.00-20.00; Saturday 10.00-13.00,
14.00-17.00
Closed: Sunday, Public Holidays.
Tube: Stratford
Bus: 25, 86, 169A
P. 58, 79

Peckham Rye Park, SE15, Tel: 693
3791.
British Rail: Peckham Rye (from
Victoria)
Bus: 12, 12A, 37, 63, 184, P3
P. 50, 57

**Percival David Foundation of Chinese
Art,** 53 Gordon Square, WC1, Tel: 387
3909.
Open: Monday 14.00-17.00; Tuesday-
Friday 10.30-17.00; Saturday
10.30-13.00
Closed: Sunday, Bank Holidays and
Saturdays preceding Bank Holidays
Tube: Marble Arch
Bus: 1, 2, 2B, 13, 26, 30, 74, 74B,
113, 159 (to Portman Square); 6, 7, 8,
12, 15, 73, 137, 500, 505, 616 (to
Selfridge's)
P. 94

Petticoat Lane, Middlesex Street, E1.
Open: Sunday morning
Tube: Aldgate, Aldgate East,
Liverpool Street
Bus: 5, 6, 8, 9A, 10, 15, 22, 23, 25,
35, 40, 42, 44, 47, 48, 78, 95, 97, 149,
243, 253
P. 73

Pharmaceutical Society's Museum, 17
Bloomsbury Square, WC1, Tel: 405
8967.
Open: by arrangement only

Tube: Holborn
Bus: 68, 77, 77A, 77B, 77C, 170, 172, 188, 196, 239, 501
P. 97
Pitshanger Manor, Ealing Public Library, Walpole Park, Ealing, W5
Tube: Ealing Broadway
Bus: 65, 83, 112, 207, 273, 274, E1, E2
P. 66
Pollocks Toy Museum, 1 Scala Street, W1, Tel: 636 3452.
Open: Monday-Saturday 10.00-17.00
Closed: Sunday, Bank Holidays
Tube: Goodge Street
Bus: 1, 14, 24, 29, 73, 176
P. 51, 108, 109-10
Portobello Road Market, W10.
Open: fruit, vegetables, flowers daily; antiques Saturday only
Tube: Ladbroke Grove, Notting Hill Gate
Bus: 7, 15, 52
P. 32, 40, 44, 71, 73
Post Office Tower, Maple Street, W1, Tel: 636 3133.
Open: Monday-Friday 9.30-21.30; Saturday, Sunday 9.00-21.30; Good Friday 11.00-21.30
Closed: Christmas Day
Tube: Great Portland Street, Warren Street
Bus: 14, 18, 24, 27, 29, 30, 73, 134, 137, 176, 253
P. 117-8
Pottery Lane, W11.
Tube: High Street Kensington, Holland Park
Bus: 9, 9A, 12, 27, 28, 31, 33, 49, 73, 88
P. 94
Pre-School Playgroups Association, 87A Borough High Street, SE1, Tel: 407 7815.
P. 95
Prince Henry's Room, 17 Fleet Street, EC4.
Open: Monday-Friday 13.45-17.00; Saturday 13.45-16.30
Closed: Sunday, Good Friday, Christmas Day
Tube: Temple

144

Bus: 4, 6, 9, 9A, 11, 15, 171, 502, 513
P. 66
Public Record Office and Museum, Chancery Lane, WC2, Tel: 405 0741.
Open: Monday-Friday 13.00-16.00; organised parties at other times by arrangement.
Closed: Saturday, Sunday, Bank Holidays
Tube: Chancery Lane, Temple
Bus: 4, 6, 9, 9A, 11, 15, 171, 502, 513
P. 33

Quainton Railway Society, David Alexander, 100 Brunswick Road, W5.
P. 113
Queen Anne's Gate, Westminster, SW1
Tube: St James's Park
Bus: 11, 24, 29, 39, 503
P. 66
Queen Elizabeth Hall, South Bank, SE1, Tel: 928 3191.
Tube: Charing Cross, Waterloo
Bus: 1, 1A, 4, 68, 70, 76, 149, 168A, 171, 176, 188, 196, 239, 501, 502, 505, 507, 513
P. 14
Queen's Chapel of the Savoy, Savoy Hill, Strand, WC2.
Open: Tuesday-Friday (during the middle of the day)
Closed: throughout August, Boxing Day
Tube: Charing Cross, Strand, Temple
Bus: 1, 1A, 4, 6, 9, 9A, 11, 13, 15, 68, 77, 77A, 77B, 77C, 109, 155, 168, 170, 171, 172, 176, 184, 188, 196, 239, 502, 505, 513
P. 11, 67
Queen's Gallery, Buckingham Palace Road, SW1.
Open: Tuesday-Saturday, Easter Monday, Spring and Late Summer Holiday Mondays 11.00-17.00, Sundays 14.00-17.00 (during exhibitions only)
Closed: between exhibitions, Good Friday, Christmas Day, Boxing Day
Tube: Victoria
Bus: 2, 2B, 10, 11, 16, 24, 25, 26, 29, 36, 36A, 36B, 38, 39, 52, 149, 181,

185, 500, 503, 506, 507
P. 26, 84
Queen's House, Greenwich *see*
National Maritime Museum
P. 66
Queen's Park Rangers F.C., Loftus
Road, W12, Tel: 743 3478;
(Supporters' Club) 743 0339.
P. 60
Questers' Theatre, Mattock Lane, Ealing,
W5, Tel: 567 5184
P. 108

Ramblers' Association, 124 Finchley
Road, NW3, Tel: 794 5611.
P. 119
Regent's Park, NW1; Open Air Theatre,
Tel: 486 2431.
Tube: Baker Street, Regent's Park,
Great Portland Street, Camden Town
Bus: 1, 2, 2B, 3, 13, 18, 26, 27, 30,
39, 53, 59, 74, 74B, 113, 137, 159, 176
P. 9, 18, 29, 57, 88, 108
Richmond Park, Surrey.
Tube: Richmond and bus 65, 71;
Putney Bridge and bus 85
Bus: 33, 37, 72, 73
P. 19, 55, 88-9, 100, 118
Roman Bath, 5 Strand Lane, WC2.
Open: Monday-Saturday 10.00-12.30
Closed: Sunday, Good Friday,
Christmas Day
Tube: Temple
Bus: 1, 1A, 4, 6, 9, 9A, 11, 13, 15,
68, 77, 77A, 77B, 77C, 109, 155, 168,
170, 171, 172, 184, 188, 196, 139, 502,
505, 513
P. 67
Roman Fort, c/o Director Guildhall
Museum, Gillett House, Bassishaw High
Walk, Basinghall Street, EC2, Tel: 606
3030.
P. 46
Romford Library, Laurie Square,
Romford, Essex.
Tube: Newbury Park and bus 66;
Dagenham Heathway and bus 174
P. 120
Rotunda Artillery Museum, Woolwich
Common, SE18,
Tel: 854 2424.

Open: Monday-Friday 10.00-12.45;
14.00-17.00; Saturday 10.00-12.00;
14.00-17.00; Sunday 14.00-17.00 (to
16.00 October-March)
Closed: Good Friday, Christmas Day
Tube: New Cross, New Cross Gate and
bus 53
Bus: 53, 54, 75
P. 21
Royal Academy *see* Burlington House
Royal Albert Hall, Kensington Gore,
SW7, Tel: 589 8212.
Tube: South Kensington
Bus: 9, 9A, 52, 73
P. 8, 63, 78
Royal College of Music, Prince Consort
Road, SW7, Tel: 589 3643.
Open: Monday, Wednesday
10.30-16.30 (in term-time only and by
appointment with the Curator)
Closed: Vacations
Tube: South Kensington
Bus: 9, 9A, 14, 30, 39A, 45, 49, 52,
73, 74, 74B
P. 77
Royal Exchange, Cornhill, EC3.
Open: Monday-Friday 10.00-16.00;
Saturday 10.00-12.00
Closed: Sunday, Bank Holidays
Tube: Bank
Bus: 6, 8, 9, 9A, 11, 15, 21, 22, 25,
43, 76, 133, 501, 502
P. 99
Royal Festival Hall, Belvedere Road,
SE1, Tel: 928 3191.
Tube: Charing Cross, Waterloo
Bus: 1, 1A, 4, 68, 70, 76, 149, 168A,
171, 176, 188, 196, 239, 501, 502, 503,
505, 507, 513
P. 14, 76, 77
Royal Mews, Buckingham Palace Road,
SW1.
Open: Wednesday, Thursday
14.00-16.00
Closed: Royal Ascot Week (June)
Tube: Victoria
Bus: 2, 2B, 10, 11, 16, 24, 25, 26, 29,
36, 36A, 36B, 38, 39, 52, 149, 181,
185, 500, 503, 506, 507
P. 19, 84, 112
Royal Mint, EC3.
Tube: Tower Hill

Bus: 9A, 42, 78
P. 67
Royal Naval College, Park Row,
Greenwich, SE10, Tel: 858 2154.
Open: daily 14.30-17.00 (except
Thursday)
Closed: Good Friday, Christmas Eve,
Christmas Day, Boxing Day
Tube: Surrey Docks and bus 1A, 70,
108B, 188
British Rail: Maze Hill
Bus: 53, 54, 75, 177, 180, 180A, 185
P. 67
Royal Opera Arcade, Pall Mall, SW1.
Tube: Green Park, Trafalgar Square
Bus: 9, 9A, 14, 19, 22, 25, 38, 506
P. 67
Royal School of Needlework, 25
Prince's Gate, SW7, Tel: 589 0077.
P. 80
Royal Small Arms Factory, Ordnance
Road, Enfield, Middlesex, Tel:
Waltham Cross ex. 23391.
Open: by appointment only
Tube: Turnpike Lane, then bus 231
British Rail: Enfield Town (from
Liverpool Street)
P. 21
Royal Society for Prevention of
Cruelty to Animals, 105 Jermyn
Street, SW1, Tel: 930 0971
P. 19, 20
Rugby Football Union, Whitton Road,
Twickenham, Middlesex.
P. 97

St Andrew's Undershaft, Leadenhall
Street, EC3.
Tube: Aldgate
Bus: 15, 25, 95
P. 10
St Bartholomew the Great, West
Smithfield, EC1, Tel: 606 5071.
Tube: Barbican, St Paul's
Bus: 4, 8, 22, 25, 141, 277, 279, 501,
502
P. 9
St Botolph, Aldgate, EC3, Tel: 283
1670
Tube: Aldgate

Bus: 15, 25, 95
P. 8, 82
St Botolph Without, Bishopsgate, EC2,
Tel: 588 1053.
Tube: Liverpool Street
Bus: 6, 8, 8A, 22, 35, 47, 48, 78, 149
P. 76, 82
St Bride Printing Library and
Museum, St Bride Institute, Bride
Lane, EC4,
Tel: 353 4660.
Open: Monday-Friday 10.00-17.00
Closed: Saturday, Sunday, Bank
Holidays
Tube: Blackfriars
Bus: 4, 6, 9, 11, 15, 17, 45, 63, 141,
168, 168A, 502 513
P. 33
St Bride's, Fleet Street, EC4, Tel: 353
1301.
Tube: Blackfriars
Bus: 4A, 6, 9, 9A, 11, 15, 502, 513
P. 9, 76
St Clement Danes, Strand, WC2, Tel:
242 8282.
Tube: Temple
Bus: 1, 1A, 4, 6, 9, 9A, 11, 15, 68, 77,
109, 155, 168, 170, 171, 172, 176,
184, 188, 196, 239, 502, 505, 513
P. 9, 43, 99
St Dunstans-in-the-West, Fleet Street,
EC4, Tel: 242 6027
Tube: Temple
Bus: 4, 6, 9, 9A, 11, 15, 171, 502,
513
P. 43, 82
St James Garlickhythe, Garlick Hill,
EC4, Tel: 236 1719.
Tube: Mansion House
Bus: 6, 9, 9A, 11, 15, 18, 76, 95, 149,
502, 513
P. 11, 82
St James's Palace, Pall Mall, SW1.
Tube: Green Park
Bus: 9, 9A, 14, 19, 22, 38, 506
P. 6, 8, 43, 85
St James's Park, SW1.
Tube: St James's Park, Trafalgar
Square, Green Park
Bus: 3, 9, 9A, 11, 12, 14, 19, 22, 24,
25, 29, 38, 39, 53, 56, 76, 77, 77A,
77B, 77C, 88, 109, 155, 159, 168,

170, 172, 177, 184, 503, 506
P. 18, 89
St John's Gate, St John's Lane, EC1.
Tube: Barbican, Farringdon
Bus: 4, 5, 8, 17, 18, 22, 25, 45, 46,
55, 63, 168A, 221, 243, 259, 277, 279
P. 67
St Katherine Creechurch, Leadenhall
Street, EC3, Tel: 283 5733.
Tube: Aldgate
Bus: 15, 25, 95
P. 13
St Lawrence Jewry, Gresham Street,
EC2, Tel: 638 0824.
Tube: St Paul's
Bus: 4A, 6, 8, 9, 11, 15, 18, 22, 25,
141, 141A, 501, 502, 513
P. 76, 99
St Margaret's Westminster, Parliament
Square, SW1, Tel: 222 6382 see
Westminster Abbey.
P. 12
St Martin-in-the-Fields, Trafalgar
Square, WC2, Tel: 930 0089. see
National Gallery
P. 13, 76
St Mary-at-Hill, Lovat Lane, EC3, Tel:
626 4184.
Tube: Monument
Bus: 8A, 9A, 10, 21, 35, 40, 40A, 43,
44, 47, 48, 133, 501, 513
P. 12, 56
St Mary-le-Bow, Cheapside, EC2, Tel:
248 5139 see Guildhall
P. 76, 81, 99
St Mary Woolnoth, Lombard Street,
EC3, Tel: 626 9701.
Tube: Bank
Bus: 6, 8, 9, 9A, 11, 15, 21, 22, 25,
43, 76, 133, 501, 502
P. 76
St Michael-upon-Cornhill, Cornhill,
EC3, Tel: 626 8841.
Tube: Bank
Bus: 6, 8, 9, 9A, 11, 15, 21, 22, 25,
43, 76, 133, 501, 502
P. 76
St Nicholas Cole Abbey, Queen
Victoria Street, EC4,
Tel: 248 5213.
Tube: Blackfriars
Bus: 17, 45, 63, 76, 109, 141, 155,

168, 168A
P. 99
St Olave's, Hart Street, EC3.
Tube: Liverpool Street
Bus: 6, 8, 8A, 22, 35, 47, 48, 78, 149
P. 10, 56, 76
St Paul's Cathedral, St Paul's Church-
yard, Ludgate Hill, EC4, Tel: 236
4128.
Cathedral
Open: April-September daily
7.45-19.00; October-March daily
7.45-18.00 (for services only Good
Friday, Easter Sunday, Christmas Day)
Crypt, Galleries
Open: June-August Monday-Saturday
10.45-18.30; May, September Monday-
Saturday 10.45-18.00; April Monday-
Saturday 10.45-17.30; October-March
Monday-Saturday 10.45-15.30
Closed: Good Friday, Christmas Day
Tube: Mansion House, St Paul's
Bus: 4, 6, 7, 8, 9, 9A, 11, 15, 18, 22,
25, 76, 141, 501, 502, 513
P. 9, 11, 13, 14, 54, 77, 118
St Peter-upon-Cornhill, Bishopsgate
Corner, EC3, Tel: 626 9483.
Tube: Liverpool Street
Bus: 6, 8, 15, 22, 35, 47, 48, 149
P. 14
St Stephens Walbrook, EC4, Tel: 626
2277.
Tube: Bank, Cannon Street
Bus: 6, 8, 9, 9A, 11, 15, 21, 22, 25,
43, 76, 133, 501, 502
P. 76
Salisbury Hall, London Colney, Herts.
Open: Easter-September; Sundays,
July-September; Thursdays
14.00-18.00 Bank Holidays
10.30-12.30 and 14.00-17.30.
Tube: High Barnet, then bus 84
P. 111
Sarah Siddons Youth Centre, North
Wharf Road, W2, Tel: 723 0073.
P. 70
Anna Scher Children's Theatre,
Bentham Court Hall, Essex Road, N1,
Tel: 722 9835.
P. 107
J. Henry Schroder Wagg, Merchant
Bankers, 120 Cheapside, EC2.

Travel: *see* Guildhall
P. 42
Science Museum, Exhibition Road,
SW7, Tel: 589 6371.
Open: Monday-Saturday 10.00-18.00;
Sunday 14.30-18.00
Closed: Good Friday, Christmas Eve,
Christmas Day, Boxing Day
Tube: South Kensington
Bus: 14, 30, 39A, 45, 49, 74, 74B
P. 33, 43, 75, 98, 110, 111, 112, 113,
120
Sea Cadet Corps, Broadway House,
The Broadway, SW19,
Tel: 540 8222
P. 30
Second Centre, The Secretary, Drama
Centre Ltd., 176 Prince of Wales Road,
NW5, Tel: 267 1177.
P. 106
Serpentine Gallery, South Carriageway,
Kensington Gardens, W2, Tel: 402
6075.
Open: April 1-October 15 daily
11.00-dusk
Closed: between exhibitions
Tube: Lancaster Gate, Knightsbridge
Bus: 9, 9A, 52, 73
P. 26
Seymour Hall, Seymour Place, W1
Tube: Marble Arch, Marylebone,
Edgware Road
Bus: 1, 6, 7, 8, 15, 16, 18, 27, 36,
36A, 36B, 176, 616
P. 8
Shell Centre, South Bank, SE1.
Public Viewing Gallery
Open: April-October Monday-
Saturday 10.00-17.30 (with an adult if
under 14)
Tube: Waterloo
Bus: 1, 4, 68, 70, 76, 149, 168A, 171,
176, 188, 196, 501, 502, 503, 505,
507, 513
P. 118
Shooters Hill, SE18.
British Rail: Lewisham, Blackheath
(from Charing Cross, London Bridge,
Waterloo) and bus 89
Green Line: 701, 702 (from
Westminster, Victoria)
P. 89

Shrewsbury Park, SE18.
Travel: *see* Shooters Hill
P. 89, 118
Sir John Soane's Museum, 13
Lincoln's Inn Fields, WC2, Tel: 405
2107.
Open: Tuesday-Saturday 10.00-17.00
Closed: Sunday, Monday, Good
Friday, Boxing Day, throughout
August
Tube: Holborn
Bus: 8, 22, 25, 68, 77, 77A, 77C, 170,
172, 188, 196, 239, 501
P. 43, 82, 94
Smithfield Market, Charterhouse
Street, EC1.
Open: Monday-Friday 06.00-13.00
Tube: Farringdon, Barbican
Bus: 4, 5, 8, 17, 18, 22, 25, 45, 46,
55, 63, 168A, 221, 243, 259, 277, 279
P. 8, 72
South End Green, Hampstead, NW3.
Tube: Belsize Park, Hampstead
Bus: 24, 46, 63, 187, 268
P. 27
Southfields Youth Centre, 333 Merton
Road, SW18, Tel: 870 3197.
P. 121
South London Art Gallery, Peckham
Road, SE5, Tel: 703 6120.
Open: Monday-Saturday 10.00-18.00;
Sunday 15.00-18.00
Closed: between exhibitions, Good
Friday, Bank Holidays, Saturday
preceding Easter, Christmas Eve
Tube: Oval and bus 36, 36A, 36B;
Elephant and Castle and bus 12, 171
P. 26
South London Theatre Centre, 2A
Norwood High Street, West Norwood,
SE27, Tel: 670 3474.
P. 106-7
Southwark Cathedral, London Bridge,
SE1, Tel: 407 2939.
Tube: London Bridge
Bus: 8A, 10, 18, 21, 35, 40, 40A, 43,
44, 47, 48, 70, 133, 501, 513
P. 10
**Southwark and Lambeth
Archaeological Society** *see* Cuming
Museum
P. 63

Spitalfields Market, Commercial Street, E1.
Tube: Liverpool Street
Bus: 5, 6, 8, 8A, 22, 35, 47, 48, 67, 78, 97, 149
P. 57, 72
Staple Inn, Holborn, WC2.
Tube: Chancery Lane
Bus: 8, 17, 18, 22, 25, 45, 46, 171, 243, 259, 501
P. 67
Stock Exchange, Old Broad Street, EC2, Tel: 588 2355.
Visitors' Gallery
Open: Monday-Friday 10.00-15.15
Closed: Weekends, Public Holidays
Tube: Bank
Bus: 6, 8, 9, 9A, 11, 15, 21, 22, 25, 43, 76, 133, 501, 502
P. 46
Stour Valley Railway Preservation Society, T. J. Gregson, 55, Bellevue Road, Billericay, Essex.
P. 113
Streatham Common, SW16.
Rookery
Open: Daily 9.00-dusk
Tube: Brixton and bus 49, 50, 57A, 59, 109, 133, 159
Bus: 57, 95, 115, 115A, 118, 130, 181, 249
P. 18
Sydenham Wells Park, SE26.
Tube: Brixton then bus 3
British Rail: Sydenham Hill
Bus: 3, 12, 12A, 63, 108B, 122
P. 18
Syon Park, Brentford, Middlesex, Tel: 560 0881.
Open: daily 10.00-20.00
Tube: Hammersmith, then bus 267 for Brent Lea Gate
P. 56, 57

Tate Gallery, Millbank, SW1, Tel: 828 1212.
Open: Monday-Saturday 10.00-18.00; Sunday 14.00-18.00
Closed: Good Friday, Christmas Eve, Christmas Day
Tube: Vauxhall, Westminster and then bus 77B, 88; Victoria, and bus 2, 2A,

2B, 36, 36A, 36B, 181, 185
P. 26
Telephone Museum, Fleet Building, Shoe Lane, EC4, Tel: 829 3750
Open: Mon-Fri 10.00-16.30
P. 47
Television Gallery, 70 Brompton Road, SW3, Tel: 584 7011.
Open: Monday-Friday (visits by arrangement, minimum age 16 years)
Tube: Knightsbridge
Bus: 14, 30, 74, 74B, 509
P. 47
Temple, EC4.
Inner Temple Hall
Open: Monday-Friday 10.00-11.30; 14.30-16.00 (during legal terms)
Middle Temple Hall
Open: Saturday 10.00-16.00; usually also Monday-Friday 10.00-12.00, 15.00-16.30
Closed: Bank Holidays and when in use for Inn activities
Tube: Temple
Bus: 4, 6, 9, 9A, 11, 15, 171, 502, 513
P. 67-8
Temple Bar, Theobold's Park, Cheshunt, Herts.
Bus: 205, 205A, 242, 279
P. 68
Temple of Mithras, Queen Victoria Street, EC4.
Tube: Bank, Mansion House
Bus: *see* Bank of England
P. 68
Thames Barge Sailing Club, The Secretary, Miss M. Bates, 35E, Sussex Place, W2 *or* c/o National Maritime Museum.
P. 30
Thames Young Mariners, Ham Fields, Richmond, Surrey, Tel: 940 5550.
P. 39
Theatre Centre Ltd, Victor Road, NW10, Tel: 969 7959.
P. 23-4, 41, 94, 107
The Times, Public Relations Officer (for tours), Printing House Square, EC4, Tel: 236 2000.
Tube: Blackfriars
Bus: 4, 6, 9, 9A, 11, 15, 502, 513
P. 47

Tooting Common, SW17, Tel: 672 6354; Lido, Tel: 769 4226.
Tube: Tooting Bec and bus 49, 249
P. 55
Tottenham Hotspur F.C., 748 High Road, N7, Tel: 808 1020; Supporters' Club, Tel: 808 7430.
Tube: Seven Sisters and bus 97, 149, 259, 279; Wood Green and bus W3
P. 60
Totters Market, Middlesex Street, E1.
Open: Sunday 7.00-16.00
Tube: Aldgate, Aldgate East, Liverpool Street
Bus: 5, 6, 8, 9A, 10, 15, 22, 23, 35, 40, 42, 44, 47, 48, 78, 95, 97, 149, 243A, 253
P. 73-4
Tower of London, Tower Hill, EC3, Tel: 709 0765.
Open: March-October Monday-Saturday 9.30-17.00, Sunday 14.00-17.00; November-February Monday-Saturday 9.30-16.00
Closed: Sundays in winter, Good Friday, Christmas Eve, Christmas Day, Boxing Day
Ceremony of the Keys: Write to The Deputy Governor, H.M. Constable's Office, Tower of London (give choice of date)
Tube: Tower Hill
Bus: 9A, 42, 78
P. 6, 9, 10, 14, 21, 29, 44, 48, 61, 62, 68, 71
Tower Pier, nr Tower Hill, EC3, Tel: 709 9697;
Tube: Tower Hill
Bus: 9A, 42, 78
P. 29
Trafalgar Square, WC2.
Travel: *see* National Gallery
P. 14, 54, 69, 99
Trinity House, Tower Hill, EC3, Tel: 480 6601
Tube: Tower Hill
Bus: 9A, 42, 78
P. 75
Madame Tussaud's, Marylebone Road, NW1, Tel: 935 6861.
Open: April-September daily 10.00-18.30; October-March Monday-

Friday 10.00-17.30, Saturdays, Sundays and Boxing Day 10.00-18.30, Good Friday 10.00-18.30, Christmas Eve 10.00-17.00
Closed: Christmas Day
Tube: Baker Street
Bus: 1, 2, 2B, 13, 18, 26, 27, 30, 59, 74, 74B, 113, 159, 176
P. 53, 62

Unicorn Theatre Club, Great Newport Street, WC2, Tel: 240 2076.
P. 95, 108
Upminster Mill, St Mary's Lane, Upminster. Write to The Town Clerk, London Borough of Havering, Romford, Essex saying when you would like to visit
Tube: Upminster
Bus: 248
P. 120
Uxbridge Road Market, Shepherd's Bush, W12.
Tube: Shepherd's Bush, Goldhawk Road
Bus: 12, 49, 88, 117, 207
P. 74

Vallance Road Market, E1.
Tube: Whitechapel
Bus: 10, 25, 253
P. 74
Veteran Car Club of Great Britain, 14 Fitzhardinge Street, W1, Tel: 935 1661.
P. 112
Victoria and Albert Museum, Cromwell Road, SW7, Tel: 589 6371.
Open: Monday-Saturday 10.00-18.00; Sunday 14.30-18.00
Closed: Good Friday, Christmas Eve, Christmas Day, Boxing Day
Tube: South Kensington
Bus: 14, 30, 39A, 45, 49, 74, 74B
P.21, 24, 33, 43, 48, 51, 77, 80, 93, 94
Victoria Embankment Gardens, WC2.
Tube: Charing Cross, Strand, Trafalgar Square
Bus: 1, 1A, 6, 9, 9A, 11, 13, 15, 77,

77A, 77B, 77C, 176, 505
P. 27
Victoria Park, Hackney, E9.
Tube: Mile End and bus 277
Bus: 8, 8A, 106, 236
P. 18, 28, 48, 55, 57
Vintage Motor Cycle Club, The
Secretary, E. E. Thompson 28 Glover
Road, Pinner, Middlesex, Tel: 866
0964.
P. 113
Vintner's Hall, Upper Thames Street,
EC4.
Tube: Mansion House
Bus: 76
P. 11, 83

Wallace Collection, Hertford House,
Manchester Square, W1, Tel: 935
0687.
Open: Monday-Saturday 10.00-17.00;
Sunday 14.00-17.00
Closed: Good Friday, Christmas Eve,
Christmas Day
Tube: Bond Street
Bus: 2, 2B, 13, 26, 30, 59, 74, 74B,
113, 159 to Portman Square; 6, 7, 8,
12, 15, 73, 88, 137, 500, 505, 616 to
Selfridge's.
P. 21, 26, 43, 45, 94
Walthamstow Market, Walthamstow
High Street, E7.
P. 74
Walthamstow Reservoir, Ferry Lane,
N17.
(Fishing permits from Metropolitan
Water Board)
P. 19, 55
Wandsworth Common, SW18, Tel: 874
1841.
Tube: Clapham South and bus 189
Bus: 19, 49, 77, 77B, 249
P. 55
War Rooms, Whitehall, SW1.
Open: Write to Chief Clerk, Cabinet
Office, Whitehall, SW1 for visits. Two
guided tours a day, Monday-Friday at
11.00, 14.30
Closed: Weekends, Bank Holidays
Travel: *see* Houses of Parliament
P. 47

Waterlow Park, Highgate, N6, Tel: 272
2825.
Tube: Archway
Bus: 210, 271
P. 18, 89
Weekend Canoe Venture, Mick Naylor,
67 Venner Road, Sydenham, SE26,
Tel: 659 3649.
P. 39
Well Hall, Well Hall Road, Eltham,
SE9.
Tudor Barn
Open: April-September Sunday-Friday
11.00-20.00; October-March Sunday-
Friday 11.00-dusk (opens 14.00
Sundays)
Closed: Saturday, Christmas Eve,
Christmas Day, Boxing Day
British Rail: Eltham (Well Hall)
Bus: 21, 21A, 61, 89, 108, 126, 132,
161, 161A, 228
P. 69
**Wellcome Institute of the History of
Medicine,** 183 Euston Road, NW1, Tel:
387 4688.
Open: Monday-Saturday 10.00-17.00
Closed: Sunday, Bank Holidays and
Saturdays preceding Spring and Late
Summer Holiday-Mondays
Tube: Euston Square, Warren Street
Bus: 14, 18, 24, 29, 30, 73, 134, 176,
253
P. 98
Wellington Museum, Apsley House,
Hyde Park Corner, W1, Tel: 499 5676.
Open: Monday-Saturday 10.00-18.00;
Sunday 14.30-18.00
Closed: Good Friday, Christmas Eve,
Christmas Day, Boxing Day
(Children under 12 must be
accompanied by an adult)
Tube: Hyde Park Corner
Bus: 2, 2B, 9, 9A, 14, 16, 22, 25, 26,
30, 36, 36A, 36B, 38, 52, 73, 74,
74B, 137, 500
P. 45
Welsh Harp Sailing Base, Cool Oak
Lane, NW9, Tel: 202 6672.
P. 39
Wembley Stadium and Empire Pool,
Empire Way, Wembley, Middlesex, Tel:
902 1234.

Tube: Wembley Central, Wembley Park
Bus: 8, 18, 83, 92, 182, 297
P. 11, 12, 78, 96, 104
Wesley's Chapel and House, City Road,
EC1, Tel: 253 2262.
Chapel
Open: daily 8.00-dusk
House
Open: Monday-Saturday 10.00-13.00;
14.00-16.00
Closed: Sunday, Bank Holidays
Tube: Old Street
Bus: 5, 43, 55, 76, 104, 133, 141,
214, 243, 271
P. 54
West Ham Stadium, Custom House,
E16.
Tube: Plaistow and bus 262
Bus: 175
P. 76
West Ham United F.C., Boleyn
Ground, Green Street, E13, Tel: 472
0704; Supporters' Club, Tel: 472 7352.
Tube: Upton Park
Bus: 5, 15, 23, 40, 58, 162, 238
P. 60
Western District Sorting Office, 35
Rathbone Place, W1, Tel: 580 3010 ex.
218.
Open: telephone to arrange party
visits, Monday-Thursday 14.30-19.30
Tube: Tottenham Court Road
Bus: 1, 7, 8, 14, 24, 25, 29, 73, 176
P. 47
Westminster Abbey, Broad
Sanctuary, SW1
Open: daily Thursday-Tuesday
8.00-18.00; Wednesday 9.20-20.00
Chapels and Ambulatory
Open: Monday and Thursday
9.20-16.00; Tuesday and Friday
10.00-16.00; Wednesday 9.20-20.00;
Saturday 9.20-14.00; 15.45-17.00
(services only Good Friday, Christmas
Day, Boxing Day)
Tube: Westminster, St James's Park
Bus: 3, 11, 12, 24, 29, 39, 53, 59, 76,
77, 77A, 77B, 77C, 88, 109, 155, 159,
168, 170, 172, 184, 503
P. 9, 12, 13, 14, 21, 33, 54, 62, 64, 82
Westminster Cathedral, Ashley Place,
SW1, Tel: 834 7452.

Open: daily 06.00-21.00; Good Friday
and Easter Saturday 9.00-21.00; Easter
Sunday and Christmas Eve 5.30-21.00;
Easter Monday, Spring and late
Summer Holiday Mondays 7.00-21.00;
Christmas Day 5.30-16.30; Boxing Day
7.00-16.30; Easter Saturday and
Christmas Eve midnight mass from
22.00
Tube: Victoria
Bus: 2, 2B, 10, 11, 16, 24, 25, 26, 29,
36, 36A, 36B, 38, 39, 52, 149, 181,
185, 500, 503, 506, 507
P. 118
Westminster Pier, Victoria
Embankment, SW1, Tel: 930 2074.
Tube: Westminster
Bus: 3, 11, 12, 24, 29, 39, 53, 59, 76,
77, 88, 109, 155, 159, 168, 170, 172,
184, 503
P. 29
White City Stadium, Wood Lane, W12,
Tel: 743 7220.
Tube: White City
Bus: 72, 105, 220, 295
P. 28, 96
Whitechapel Art Gallery, High Street,
E1, Tel: 247 1492.
Open: telephone for details of
exhibition hours
Tube: Aldgate East
Bus: 5, 10, 15, 23, 25, 40, 40A, 67,
253
P. 26
Whitefriars Glassworks (Mrs Green for
visits), Tudor Road, Wealdstone,
Middlesex,
Tel: 427 1527
British Rail: Harrow and Wealdstone
(from Euston)
P. 47
Whitestone Pond, Hampstead, NW3
Tube: Hampstead
Bus: 210, 268
P. 87, 118
William Morris Gallery, Lloyd Park,
Forest Road, Walthamstow, E17, Tel:
527 5544.
Open: October-March Monday-
Saturday 10.00-13.00; 14.00-17.00;
April-September Tuesday, Thursday
10.00-13.00; 14.00-20.00; first Sunday

in month 10.00-12.00; 14.00-17.00
(not Easter Sunday)
Closed: Good Friday, Bank Holidays,
Saturday preceding Easter Sunday
Tube: Walthamstow Central
Bus: 34, 55, 69, 123, 262, 275, 276,
W21
P. 27, 33, 80, 94
**Wimbledon Common and Putney
Heath,** SW19.
Tube: Putney Bridge, and Bus: 74,
85, 85A, 93; Wimbledon and bus 93
Bus: 28, 72, 168
P. 48, 62, 89-90, 120
Wimbledon Stadium, Plough Lane,
SW17,
Tel: 946 5361.
Tube: Wimbledon, Tooting Broadway
and Express Bus
Bus: 44, 77, 77A, 77B, 77C, 189, 220
P. 76
Windsor Castle, Windsor, Berks,
Tel: Windsor 63106
Open: (telephone to check times
before visit as the Castle is sometimes
closed when people are staying there,
and opening times vary)
Normal Opening: May-September
Monday-Saturday 11.00-17.00, Sunday
13.30-17.00; October-April Monday-
Saturday 11.00-15.00 (or 16.00)
Closed: Sundays in winter, 11 March-6
May, 4 June-1 July, 9 December-
8 January (these dates vary)
British Rail: Windsor (from Waterloo)

Green Line Coach: 704, 705 (from
Victoria)
P. 51
Woolwich Free Ferry.
Bus: 40A, 51, 51A, 53, 54, 69, 75, 96,
99, 101, 122, 122A, 124, 161, 161A,
177, 180, 180A, 192, 229
P. 30, 37
Wormwood Scrubs, W12.
Tube: East Acton, White City
Bus: 72, 105, 220, 295
P. 9, 11, 12, 28, 97

Young Coin Collectors, 2 Arundel
Street, WC2.
P. 44
Young Music Makers, 16 Golderslea,
Finchley Road, NW11, Tel: 458 6903.
P. 77
Young People's Theatre, 13 Nevada
Street, SE10, Tel: 858 4447.
P. 107
Young Vic, The Cut, Waterloo, SE1,
Tel: 928 7616.
Tube: Waterloo
Bus: 1, 1A, 4A, 68, 70, 76, 176, 188,
188A, 196, 501, 502, 504
P. 108
Youth and Music, 22 Blomfield Street,
EC2, Tel: 588 4714.
P. 77
Youth Hostel Association, 29 John
Adam Street, WC2, Tel: 839 1722.
P. 38